"*Liberation Unleashed* further docum
activity: online peer-to-peer mentoring, no aimme ....
This book helps move us from the age of the guru to the age of the friend."

> —**Greg Goode**, author of *The Direct Path* and *After Awareness*, and coauthor of *Emptiness and Joyful Freedom*

"As Ilona points out in this wonderful book, there was truly a fire started with the Liberation Unleashed movement that occurred several years ago. I remember it well, as many people flocked to the movement in order to cut a path straight to liberation. In many ways, the movement has revolutionized the way people consider liberation these days. The pointing is very direct and leaves out a lot of unnecessary spiritual stuff. I've known many people who found it to be tremendously helpful. And the fire of the movement is still burning strong with this powerful book by Ilona. Highly recommended."

> —**Scott Kiloby**, CEO of The Kiloby Center for Recovery

"In this book, Ilona's honesty and integrity shine through. In a world of gurus vying for your devotion and money, Ilona's new book is refreshingly different. In ordinary language, completely free of pretense, she invites you to take a look for yourself and discover whether your assumptions are true. She skillfully guides you through an investigation that may reveal a shocking clarity that you are not what you thought. I enjoyed this book."

> —**Joey Lott**, author of *The Best Thing That Never Happened*

liberation
unleashed

A Guide to Breaking Free from
the Illusion of a Separate Self

ILONA CIUNAITE

NON-DUALITY PRESS
An Imprint of New Harbinger Publications

Publisher's Note

Distributed in Canada by Raincoast Books

Copyright © 2016 by Ilona Ciunaite
        Non-Duality Press
        An imprint of New Harbinger Publications, Inc.
        5674 Shattuck Avenue
        Oakland, CA 94609
        www.newharbinger.com

Cover design by Amy Shoup

Library of Congress Cataloging-in-Publication Data

Names: Ciunaite, Ilona, author.
Title: Liberation unleashed : a guide to breaking free from the illusion of a
  separate self / Ilona Ciunaite.
Description: Oakland, CA : Non-Duality, 2016.
Identifiers: LCCN 2016017899 (print) | LCCN 2016033385 (ebook) | ISBN
  9781626258068 (paperback) | ISBN 9781626258075 (pdf e-book) | ISBN
  9781626258082 (epub) | ISBN 9781626258075 (PDF e-book) | ISBN
  9781626258082 (ePub)
Subjects: LCSH: Mind and body. | Self. | Spiritual life. | BISAC: BODY, MIND
  & SPIRIT / General. | RELIGION / Eastern. | SELF-HELP / Spiritual.
Classification: LCC BF161 .C458 2016 (print) | LCC BF161 (ebook) | DDC
  202/.2--dc23
LC record available at https://lccn.loc.gov/2016017899

18   17   16

10   9   8   7   6   5   4   3   2   1   First Printing

Your heart and my heart are very, very old friends.

—Hafiz

This book is dedicated to *you*.

Contents

Preface

Dear Reader,

Are you looking for something? Do you wish that life was different, more joyful, and free? Do you feel a longing for something—even though you may not know what that "something" might be? Are you on a mission to improve yourself, or are you looking for the way to end suffering? I was looking for answers, too, and what I found was so surprising and simple that I have to share it with you.

A Little Bit about Ilona

I was born in Lithuania. For the past nineteen years I have lived in England. I am happily married to a man whom I met when I was twenty-one. He was a tattoo artist when I met him. I learned the craft from him and became a tattoo artist too. We have a little custom-tattoo studio. I enjoy drawing on skin, creating beautiful designs, and meeting people from every walk of life. If you would like to see some of my tattoo work, you can go to www.mantas-tattoo.com.

The First Disillusionment

Once I was a little girl, and I believed in Santa. I also believed in a magical fairy friend and a little devil named "Number 13" who could make things happen for me. I think I was about seven when the first illusion crashed. My friend Sandra told me that Santa was not real and that it was my parents who put the gifts under the Christmas tree. I wanted to cry. It was unbelievable, and I argued with her for a bit. She insisted that my parents had lied. I couldn't believe it, but she was right. This was big. The magic world was breaking down and I saw that parents lie. I could not believe that they had tricked me. The whole illusion, that Senis Šaltis (the Lithuanian name for him) came and left us all these presents, had been so convincing. With one look at reality my belief in magic had been shattered! And it was gone for good. Since then, no one could possibly convince me that Santa is this guy who lives at the North Pole and brings presents to all the good kids all over the world on one magical night. Yeah, imagine that!

Time passed, and I grew up and picked up beliefs about everything. Some of them seemed quite magical, including new age teachings about the Higher Self and so forth.

Looking for Truth

The searching for the truth started on one magic night in 2002. I experienced silence of the thinking mind, a sweet sense of being, contentment, peace, and feeling at home. That magic-mushroom trip was the beginning of my journey to find home. I wanted to reach that state again, where all was felt as one, stillness, just being, and the sweetness of bliss. I then spent several months searching the Internet, just like Neo in *The Matrix*, looking for clues, reading all kinds of stuff, and wanting to understand what had happened. A lot of anger came up. I could not believe that no one had told me about this state of being.

To tell the truth, I was a lazy seeker. I read a few books but never went to any meetings, retreats, or groups. I had not heard of satsangs, had never met a teacher or a guru. I was alone in this search most of the time; at one point I had a friend who would talk about spiritual stuff and share thoughts about books that I read. I liked the authors Osho and Richard Bach.

Trying Out Some Paths

I loved experimenting with different modalities, especially sound healing, binaural beats, Holosync, and so forth. It was easy to get into deep states with the help of technology, particularly as I did not have the patience to meditate. I would put headphones on and let the frequencies take me away. Most of the time I just fell asleep. I tried many things for fun and exploration.

It took eight years and many bumps in the road for me to arrive at Jed McKenna's books about spiritual enlightenment and the search for truth. I read all three of his books in two weeks during

Easter of 2010 and got a real shock to the belief system. Jed cata-pulted me out of hypnosis. By "hypnosis" I mean following other people, looking for truth in what others were saying, believing this and that, and trying to fix my beliefs as if that would give me a happy tomorrow. As Richard Bach says in his book *Hypnotizing Maria*, a suggestion accepted is hypnotism. I accepted suggestions from everyone and everything around me: friends, parents, media, school, university, books, movies.

Deconstruction, Pain, and Peace

Then I realized that I had no idea that I had no idea. I thought I knew things and could make the universe dance to my own tune. I tried to believe in my ability to control, but somehow deep within it felt like a lie. What a sick joke.

The deconstruction of my castle of bullshit had started. I was looking at concepts and finding nothing but beliefs about beliefs and thoughts about thoughts—lots of them—all built up to form that castle. I was doing as Jed McKenna suggested, writing it all down, looking at what I knew was true. I was slowly coming out of the fog of following others and learning to think for myself, to see more clearly.

Some four months of deep depression followed: crying almost every day, seeing the hopelessness of my condition and of the condi-tion of humanity, facing lie after lie, attacking belief after belief, seeing how everyone I knew was in a trance of suffering and hoping for things to change for the better. This was a painful time. Facing the fact that no belief is true was not easy, but it had to be done. I could not stop at halfway anymore. Beliefs about truth needed to go. Truth needed to be seen, recognized, felt, and known deeply. Only then, only when this initial deconstruction was done with, could I relax.

The depression ended at last and, finally, I felt at peace. There was an emptiness, a not knowing, a not believing anything about anything. I could no longer say the words "I believe" in a conversation because I knew it was all a lie. It was so obvious to me that the word "believe" holds a lie within it: be-*lie*-ve. I could no longer share lies disguised as sacred truths. Questioning beliefs felt like ripping pieces from myself. After cutting many lies out of the system, one last step remained.

This is when I found the online forum called Ruthless Truth, created by Ciaran Healy. The one message there was, "There is no *you*, look!" The directness of the message was striking. The conviction of people on the forum seemed odd but made me curious. In unison they were all saying, "Just take a fucking look!"

So, I looked...

It's so obvious. There is no separate self at all—it's all one! One movement of one life, one reality, one this. Not even "one," just *this*. There is no separate avatar inside this body driving it, no ghost in the machine. Just life. Just this immediate experiencing, flowing freely, plain and simple.

And that was it. For a moment I felt astonishment. The first thought that came was, *How did I never question that before?!* The absence of a self is in plain sight, and yet it is the least obvious thing to question. I didn't receive a cosmic download or hear an angel choir with this realization. No bright lights shone in my eyes, nor did I receive a medal for achievement. I smiled, felt disbelief at how simple it is, and one more magic fairy tale fell away.

I scratched my head and thought, *Wow! No more belief in separation from life, from the source. No more delusion about Ilona running the show. Ha! No one is driving the show.* The show did not stop, it was seen as just happening. The line was crossed. Then, the falling started. More beliefs came up and went, then even more and more. The most precious truths seemed the hardest to relinquish, but somehow, all the clearing became effortless as I realized that holding on to ideas and concepts is of no use.

The End of the Search, but Not the End of the Journey

The journey carried on, but the seeker was no longer there. Well, she never was there, just some story that was being told over and over again that was believed to be the truth of how things were.

Months went by and I noticed how searching had dropped and how opinions—mine or anyone else's—no longer mattered. I noticed how everything was the same old, same old, but at the same time it was fresh, intimate, immediate, and raw. There was a sense of freedom, sweetness, and joy that arose. For some months I lived in bliss; I was high on life. I could not sleep but felt rested, I could not eat but felt full. I felt a lot of energy.

A Beginning

I still had the sense of a mission, that something needed to be done. This did not drop away. I started writing the blog *Marked, Eternal*, sharing thoughts about this newfound freedom and inviting readers to look, for themselves, into their own experience. With my dearest friend, Elena, I was stirring the pot in some Facebook groups, pointing to non-separatedness, and encouraging people to take a look, using what we call Direct Pointing.

The Direct Pointing method consists of a dialogue between a guide and a seeker. It is a process of looking at *what is* with no requirement for prior knowledge or years of seeking. The guide poses very specific questions to the seeker in order to focus the attention on the experience of the present moment. This triggers what we refer to as "crossing the Gateless Gate," an instant in which the illusion of a separate self is seen through. A shift in perception happens. People who have crossed the Gateless Gate may become guides and pose to seekers the same questions that they themselves once tried to answer.

It wasn't just Elena and I who started Direct Pointing, there was a group of us from the Ruthless Truth forum who were passionately ringing wake-up bells and whistling, inviting people to simply *look*.

People started writing to us in private. We had many e-mail conversations in which others came to see the absence of the entity "I." (All those conversations are published on my blog.) This process was exhilarating, exciting; it felt revolutionary. Each time someone else recognized the absence of "I," it felt like seeing it for the first time, again and again. That was really heart opening. It still is, as I have never stopped working with people, pointing to no self.

Liberation Unleashed

In September 2011, with help of Elena Nezhinsky and Ciaran Healy, Liberation Unleashed (LU) was created as an independent sister forum to the now-defunct Ruthless Truth. LU came to life with a big bang. On the night the website went live, Elena's house in New York burned down. The launch of the forum seared an extraordinary memory in our minds—how much fire there was at the beginning of this movement, how much burning intensity for truth and compassion for fellow humans searching for the way out of suffering. It felt as if a mighty wall had been breached and that there was a crack in the foundation. There was finally a way to make a difference, a real change in human life. It seemed that this change in perception would open up the doors for so much more. All we did was point. We held up the Exit sign and made a noise, knowing that those who had ears to hear it would come and look for themselves. And they did.

I have had hundreds of conversations with people from all around the globe over the past few years. Some saw the illusion of "I" quickly, some not so quickly, and some were not ready. Each individual's process was unique, and it took as long as it took. I have continued pointing since the launch. I've integrated it into my life as a daily, routine job. I hold live meetings and group sessions in the town where I live. All of my work is on *Marked, Eternal* and the LU forum, including the recordings of my meetings with individuals. It has been quite a journey, and I am enjoying every minute of it. I feel immense gratitude for everyone involved in this unique project. Thank you, too.

It's Closer Than You Think

To tell you the truth, my story is irrelevant. This book is not about me and my realizations. It doesn't matter how I describe what I see. I'm not going to tell you about my experiences or how to reach the state where I am. I'm just going to point for you, relentlessly, so that you can see it too. When seeing happens, words are no longer necessary. They can be here, or not. Once recognized, it cannot be unrecognized.

It's not even hidden.

It's closer than you think.

Literally.

So, let's start and get right to the point!

The Word "I" Is a Tool for Communication— Nothing More

There is no such separate entity or self who is in charge behind the word "I." "I" is a thought—a thought that is useful in a conventional way when communicating. It is not "I" who is communicating. It is not "I" who is reading these words.

It is not "I" who is writing this, either.

When I say "I," it is meant as a tool of communication in the form of language. It is not referring to the individual me who is thinking and writing.

How to Use This Book

You can read this book in different ways: from beginning to end or just picking a chapter that resonates the most in the moment and working with the questions suggested there. Along the way I share some of the conversations I had with people who wrote to me. Or you can jump right to the end of the book and start with the seven steps, then read relevant chapters if you get stuck.

Set Time for Writing Down Thoughts on Paper Every Day

It's a good idea to set aside time each day to do the exercises using a writing pad. There are two things that I would like to mention:

Writing helps the mind to focus.

Writing every day builds momentum.

When you work with the exercises and the questions presented in them, write all your thoughts down so you can see what thoughts and beliefs are there; it's easier to deal with them when they are written down on paper. Question everything, and don't just write questions, but answer them. Answer them for yourself, from your own thinking—not from what you read, what you think, or what you believe—but notice what is actually true in experience. Your experience. What do you really know? What do you really want? This book is your journey deeper into what is and out of what isn't.

This is my journey too. I thank you deeply for joining me here.

Quit Following

I did not read a *lot* of books while I was seeking for answers to my never-ending questions about what is actually happening; however, I read a few—some great ones too. The books that had the biggest effect on me were the ones that told me to think for myself. I realized I took other people's descriptions of how things are to be the truth; they seemed to know something I did not and tried to teach me this or that. I followed methods, advice, prescriptions; I tried a few things, only to see that following a method does not work. Nothing seemed to work. *Until I quit following.*

I discovered that all the beliefs I had were nice stories that *seemed* true. I also saw how the usual learning-teaching method worked; it is based on the "repeat after me" principle. I realized that I had not been using my own mind; instead I had made assumptions about what was true from what I was told, what I read, or what I saw on a screen. Using my own head to answer my own questions in the beginning was difficult and rather strange, but at the same time it was also fun. It was much more interesting than comparing who said what. I felt like I had found a muscle that I didn't know was there and I had never used or exercised.

This is where you have to let go of all that you know to be true, all that you expect and hope for. I will guide you to look, step by step. You will see for yourself, and *know* rather than understand, that there is no separation from life, from all that is. You'll realize that "I" is a thought, not an entity, that a separate self does not exist. All you need to do in order to see this is to look. Simply look at what you think that "I" is. This is what I'm going to point you to. Little by little, pieces of the puzzle will fall into place, and the view will be revealed.

Each chapter is a small piece. It's up to you to connect the dots, do the math, and resolve the question of self once and for all.

Here is my invitation to you: stop reading about, listening to, and watching what someone else has to say about your burning questions. Find out what is true, and inquire until you know—till all is clear. Do this for yourself, by yourself, for the love of truth.

I invite you to put all beliefs aside and to take a fresh look. Don't just read my words, retest them. Is something true in actual experience? How do you know? What else do you notice?

Questions arise to be dissolved; they dissolve when they no longer make sense. Getting all the answers is not what you want; what you want is to have no more questions. Mind wants answers; the mind needs to know and to explain; it likes theories, models, and philosophy.

So, when spiritual and religious teachers say how it is—what it is like for them, what states they experience, what works and what doesn't—that's all about *their* experience, not yours. You can only know what is true for you. Trying to compare only creates speculation and expectation. That is what distorts the view. And if you can see something clearly, you can describe it in your own words.

Trust that what you need is already here. The next step that you need to take will present itself. Follow your own path—you are already on it. Enough of listening to more descriptions; dive into experience and explore what is happening as it's happening.

When your friend eats an apple and describes how sweet it tastes, how fragrant it is, how crunchy the flesh feels, how can you know what he is talking about if you haven't tasted that apple? The description of experience is no help when it comes to the sense of experiencing. We can talk about tasting the apple, but it's all conceptual: ideas about ideas and not the experience that is happening right now. Ideas are good for directing attention, like this: The next time you eat an apple, remember to experience the taste fully, as if you are tasting the apple for the first time. Dive into the experience, noticing all and forgetting all you know about the apple. Savor every bite of it. See the difference between talking about the taste of the apple and tasting it.

Your Best Guides Are Fear and Resistance— and Excitement

Fear and resistance come to show you the way through what is ready to be explored. Fear and resistance work together as a protective mechanism, a signal to not go somewhere unknown, unsafe, or dark. But, in experience, this signal is only a sensation triggered by thoughts. This sensation is not to be feared. Just as any other sensation, it comes and goes. It is felt as raw energy. When felt fully it dissipates. Explore it with curiosity, as if you have never seen it before. Ultimately, fear and resistance are sensations that prevent us from going into another sensation. Sensations are not to be feared; they are here to be experienced. And even if they are uncomfortable, they add a richness and juiciness to life.

Excitement is the other side of fear and resistance, and it's another great guide. It's inviting, adventurous, and joyful, whereas fear and resistance are made up of closure, insecurity, feeling out of control, and contraction. If something excites and interests you, wakes up your curiosity with a feeling of childlike innocence— follow up on your curiosity, play with it.

You already have all you need to go on this journey. Burn the maps and draw your own; put away all the expectations. For the time being, take a sabbatical from social media and computer games—just for a while. Focus on the focusing itself. Find the observer, and look for yourself—the one who you apparently are.

Your direction is here now. But wait, you are already here, right here, right now. Here it *is*. That is your path. Go deeper into the now.

Be Aware of Distraction

When you almost see through beliefs, distractions may become very tempting. Distraction is another protective mechanism that works to take your focus away from even the possibility of changing your current perspective. The old existing view is being protected, as if it's something that is owned and can be damaged. It's as if an invisible shield of certainty is being threatened.

The current view is temporary. If it is not changing, there is stagnation. If the view is not changing, the train is not moving. There is no final view, so holding on to the current view is not a positive course of action. Distractions come hurrying in to keep the belief system as it is. Sometimes it may seem difficult to hold focus. Just be aware that this scenario may play itself out.

Distractions often come as sudden impulses to do something else. Something comes up with a sense of urgency—a pull to engage in some other activity that moves you away from investigation. It is okay, of course, to follow that impulse and get distracted. It is also okay to notice it and keep focusing. Don't take the distractions seriously, just note when they show up and see what is behind them. What is being protected?

The I Virus

When I first saw that the "I," the "me," the alleged General Manager, the doer and thinker, the Command Center of the Universe is an idea that does not exist as I thought it did, I looked around and described what I saw. The best way I could paint a word picture was to use the image of a computer virus. I could see how this belief in separateness distorts the view of what is happening; I could see how much it affects human life. I could see how this belief in separateness is not necessary, how it is diminishing the whole experience of life to a contracted, ill, uneasy, and tiny space—a painful place, one that feels wrong. This thinking is like a prison without a door. I saw the simplicity of life and the struggle and difficulty it takes to see it, when all the while it is right in front of our noses, as close as it gets, the obviousness of what is.

I wrote down what I saw and named this disease of the human condition the "I Virus."

Don't take it too seriously. It is just a metaphor.

Imagine life as an organic computer system governed by software, in which each piece of hardware is run by a specific program. All cats behave like cats, as their programming dictates. All monkeys behave like monkeys, and all humans behave like humans—only the human software has been corrupted by the I Virus.

The I Virus corrupts the very core of the program, the main intelligence, the organizing structure. Human beings have lost direct access to the intelligence program, even though connectedness and oneness are the natural ways of being.

The I Virus overrides the program, and as a result the infected human thinks that it is the "I," the person, the self who owns and runs his separate piece of life. He assumes the self is something real, something special and very important that must survive. Infected humans feel disconnected from life, and they can be destructive to themselves and the environment.

The I Virus installs itself early in childhood, bypassing the immune system so there is not even a shadow of a doubt in any human's thinking (software) that there is an "I" at all. Because "I" makes itself at home in the mind, it is taken to be the organism's default program. The virus is a bit like Windows, OS X, or Linux—an operating system.

"I" exists in the mind as a separating agent. Resistance to *what is*, is the signature behavior of the I Virus. From an infected point of view, there is "I" on one side and everything else on the other side. One, separate from all, disconnected from everything else, in opposition to all; one who needs to fight for survival. One who needs to always be right, in control, safe, accepted, and loved.

Imagine that you put your finger in the ocean; you take it out and there is a drop of water hanging off your fingertip. You give the drop a name and a story. That's a separate entity now, a "me" that thinks, *I'm a drop, I'm not the ocean, and I am the nicest, most important drop. Look at me, me, me, me.* This is what the story of a separate entity, an "I," looks like: a separated self who owns his or her story— past, present, and future. An "I" who lives life and makes things happen. An "I" who has problems and little time to solve them.

The Symptoms

If you see yourself as a separate being to whom life is happening, as one who is trying to keep everything under control, you are infected. If you think that something is wrong with you or the world around you, you have the I Virus. It can show up as fearful thoughts and worries about how you are too much of this and too little of that; it makes you think life is unfair and that all should be different. If you are trying to escape your present conditions and are looking for a happy tomorrow, you have the I Virus.

The I Virus is very clever; it attaches itself to your very core, to the operating system files of human software, and creates a lens through which humans see the world. It becomes the master organizer of experience, and it's through this process that suffering begins as the never-ending illusion of "not enough" in varying degrees and stages. Suffering mixes a cocktail from the heavy emotions of sadness, hopelessness, despair, clinging, shame, anger, and guilt. You name it. And as you drink that cocktail, you end up feeling like *I don't want this, get me out of here! Not again... Why me?*

Infected humans live in constant frustration, fighting unwanted intense emotions. Their main fears are of death, nothingness, nonexistence, lack of control, pain, and bad things happening in the future. From these, other fears are spawned, and, like a spider's web, fear connects to all areas of the infected human's life. Another great fear is, paradoxically, the fear of life, the fear of living and loving freely.

Self-centered humans always feel like something is wrong with them. They compare their assumed selves to other assumed selves and try to become better, improved, and more like someone else all the time. The feeling of wrongness comes from the deep knowing that there is no separation, but the I Virus never allows any kind of questioning of the existence of "I." It's just not in the programming. Such questioning can't happen by accident.

Infected humans know that there is something wrong with the "me," but they do not see what it is exactly. They think that happiness is connected to the quality of "I," so they try to improve themselves, to become a better I, an I who is always right and wise beyond measure. They think that they have an ego; they feel that happiness is somewhere outside, that it has to come from someone or something else, that there is someone or something out there that can give it to them—and that they have a right to it, whatever it is.

What do humans infected with the I Virus want the most? Attention, energy from others, praise, compassion, understanding, love, and...peace, even though there is a great fear of peace. Peace, in fact, feels threatening.

The Antidote

The antidote to this madness is truth. Truth is seen by looking at experience, at what is actually happening right here, right now, *in* experience, underneath all thoughts.

After the Antidote

Humans who become free of the virus are plugged back into the main power supply—life. They no longer need to feed on the energy of other humans. Some people call this "enlightenment." I'd say it's more like en-Life-enment.

Once *enlifened*, humans slowly or suddenly come back to their natural state, free from neediness and dissatisfaction, and find themselves out of the drama, out of "not enough," and look around with fresh eyes. Everything is the same but looks different. There is lightness and a feeling as if some heavy baggage was dropped. The story changes. Truth is realized. Truth is recognized. The symptoms of the I Virus start to loosen up and eventually, in time, disappear.

More About the Virus

Let's imagine for a second (please don't take this too seriously) that the I Virus is a small code that attaches itself, unnoticed, to the core human life program, just like a malicious computer program that gets into the operating system without your knowledge and damages the machine. Some computer viruses can replicate themselves and use a lot of memory, bringing the system to a halt. Some attach to your e-mails and spread to other machines, bypassing security. In a similar way, the I Virus takes control of the Infinite Intelligence Program (life itself) and makes the host think that he or she is a separate self. This new "self" comes with the illusion of free choice.

In natural life, what is free choice? For example, there is the seed of a tree containing a genetic code that activates itself when the requirements and conditions for growth are met—soil, water, heat, light, air. The seed contains all of the tree's information, which is deployed at the right time. Now what choice does the tree have? To be a tree or to not be a tree...? A tree is always a tree, not a bee or a bird. In whatever form or shape the tree comes, it is dependent upon genetic code and environmental conditions.

How Do You Know You're Infected?

Infected humans think that they are self-regulating managers who can manipulate life and have independent choice. These people think that it is up to them to decide what they are and what they want to be. They compare themselves to others and follow those they want to emulate. Whole fashions and followings are born. Suffering arises when a voice in the head says, *I have a choice.* But life shows us that it is not like that. No matter what humans want, all they can ever get is what life brings to this present moment.

Choices like whether or not to have a pizza or a green smoothie are just preferences determined by past experience in a given situation. Everything is dependent on everything else. Choices to study or to work are not up to the human; they are decided by the pattern, by the software code that runs the human. Skills and talents are not up to the human; no matter how much one likes to sing, if talent is not there, the song may be a funny noise or an annoying sound (as seen on TV talent shows). Only infected humans feel that independent choice is real. The free human completely surrenders to what is and is at peace with the flow of life. He or she no longer sees separation. Actions are taken without owning them. Everything that happens is okay.

Infected humans cannot control life, even though they believe deeply that they can and that they must be able to. One day, they hope, everything will be just as they want it. Permanently. Happy forever. They will be at peace when all wishes and desires are met. It will happen one day in the happy tomorrow. The hope is so strong. The mind dreams endless what-if scenarios and creates hope and desire as well as fear—fear that a desired outcome may never happen. But if you look at nature, there is no such thing as hope. Hope is the life preserver that the drowning human tries to grab. Hope is a symptom of delusion; it's mind-fog, a glorified hypnotic thought, the opposite of hopelessness.

Infected humans want something else all the time. They *are* the flow, but the I Virus in the mind says otherwise. People want to choose what is best for themselves, but how can they ever know what is best? From the point of view of people who believe they are separate, it's definitely not *what is* that would be best for them.

How to Remove the Virus

The solution to the I Virus? The surgical removal of it, one human at a time, by running an antivirus program that goes through the files, destroying and deleting the infected parts. Then the system can be started afresh.

To start the healing, all you need to do is look with honesty and courage into the truth, into the obvious.

There is no "you" that you think you are. There is flow of life—effortless, spontaneous—happening by itself, right here, right now. Sensations are happening, thoughts are passing by; they are not your thoughts; there is no thinker. The thinker isn't someone special—the thinker is nothing but the thought.

Noticing Is Effortless

If you feel tension when trying to look at *what is*, you are trying too hard. Stop trying. Looking is a matter of noticing what is already here, not inventing or imagining something that needs a huge amount of energy to sustain. It's not mental gymnastics, and there's no medal that you have to go for. Soften, breathe—smile even. Take your time to relax and simply notice what is happening in the present: sensations, muscle tension, feelings, subtle eye movements, sounds, smells. This sort of noticing is effortless; attention moves and focuses on different perceptions, different information coming in. Thoughts rush in to label what is being noticed. No special state is required; it's everyday ordinary business.

Looking, noticing, and seeing are all the same action expressed through different words that can be used interchangeably for our purposes. If I asked you to tell me what is behind your back right now, you could answer by doing one of two things: by thinking and remembering, or by turning your head around and actually looking back and describing what you see. If I ask you to look for your phone or keys, you would quite naturally, without forcing it, take a look with your own two eyes and locate them. That's how to look.

Looking is finding out what is true in experience. It is a nonverbal action of focusing attention on a target. Thinking is verbal—it is naming experience. Both work together as one mechanism. If you can't see for yourself, you cannot describe it in your own words (but you can attempt to describe it using someone else's words, from memory).

You may say that you are trying really hard and still cannot see, and you might even ask if some people just cannot see. Ironically, *trying* to see is imagining or presupposing that you do not see—the opposite of looking at what is here already, in this very moment, right now. Of course, you already see what is here now. No effort is required: what you see is undeniable. This action is plain, simple, and ordinary. Look around.

> **Try This for Yourself** Take a little journey with me. Focus on *what is*, on direct, immediate, actual experience. Notice sensations in the hands and feet, light, and sounds; just listen, feel. Soften, allow, indulge.
>
> Let all of this be okay for a minute and a half. Whatever this is. Just sit with it, allowing all that comes up to be here. Notice sensations of being, vibration, aliveness. Are you "doing" being or is being "on" by default?
>
> Feel the sensations and see how the mind attempts to describe all that it focuses on.
>
> Notice the sensation in the left foot. There is a sensation, plus thoughts about it. Is there a feeler of sensation? Is there a feeler of feeling? Does feeling happen to another sensation? Stop reading for now and close the eyes for a bit.
>
> Now turn the attention to feeling the emotion that is most evident now. See how the mind names it. The action of labeling creates a sense of solidity and identity. But what is underneath the concepts? A raw sensation, a flow of perceiving. Be with the flow and watch what is happening. This is *what is*, in all its glorious simplicity.
>
> Can you see a difference between looking/noticing and thinking? What is the main difference? Have a look now to verify for yourself. Write it all down.

Thinking Is Not the Same as Looking

Look for your *self*, the one you supposedly are or own. And by look, I mean exactly that: Check. What *is* actually here? Like this: Touch your right ear. Touch your left foot. Touch the chair. Then touch what you call "myself." Where does a finger land?

Looking in experience can only be happening now, *not in the thoughts* about past or future. So any time you don't know where to look, bring attention back to *what is*.

Expect that this should be somehow different and... here you go, you are trying to fit *what is* into a frame of thoughts, into concepts. Is pigeonholing "what is" even possible? Soften, breathe, and look again.

The only thing to understand is that looking is not about understanding. It's about recognition.

Expectations Are Like Clouds That Cover the Sunshine

Such a lovely day on the seaside. Sunshine, light breeze, and sounds of the sea, seagulls, and distant traffic. It's delicious to sit on a bench in the sunshine and just be. This moment is complete. Nowhere to rush to. Nothing to plan. There is peace and a sense of deep joy, of being alive. The heart is wide open, streaming love.

I had a few glimpses into the gorgeousness of just being before awakening, but they were fleeting and short. The mind would start wandering and get lost in dreamy images of past and future, possibilities, and probabilities. Now I can sit and just be, without getting sucked into the story land, enjoying the view and listening to the orchestra of aliveness.

This peace and delight is underneath all judgmental thinking, and it is available at any time. But to get here one needs to leave behind all problems, hopes, and expectations the same way we leave shoes at the door upon entering our house. You may say that it's easier said than done and, of course, you are right, because even though the mind is seeking peace, it feels that peace is threatening. As if peace would mean an end to the stream of thoughts, the death of the narrator.

Expectations are the biggest obstacles to seeing this moment *as it is*. They are the shoulds and should nots, the wants and don't wants—the musts, needs, and other mind weeds. These thoughts have a pull, and once they arrive they have the power to drag one into the story and—puff! The peace is lost.

The mind creates expectations, as this is what it is used to doing; this is its job. It's a habit, an addiction. It seems obvious that everyone has expectations, plans for the future, and ideals to seek. If you don't have goals and expectations, there must be something wrong with you, right? It's so ingrained in our heads that it's not even possible to raise these questions: Do we need expectations at all? In daily, ordinary activities, in a practical sense, are expectations useful?

Have you ever wondered what it would be like to live without expectations? Well, the first thing I noticed living without expectations is that there is no more tension, nor constant need to get somewhere. The feeling of being in a hurry, of not enough time, is gone. Thoughts about time no longer feel like pressure. All that needs to be done gets done at the right time, no later or earlier. With that, all thoughts about what someone else will think if I do not deliver are gone too. Gone are the judgments and excuses that used to be popular topics in the "thought show." The mind no longer creates future scenarios in which it looks for solutions to imagined problems, to the what-ifs. It doesn't even go there, as this exercise does not add to experience but only redirects the focus to dreamland, which the mind now recognizes is futile. It can be entertaining and fun to wander into imagination, and if that's what's happening, then yes to that.

I am a tattoo artist. I used to have nightmares in which I saw people sitting and waiting in the reception area while I was busy tattooing and rushing around. The waiting people made me feel uncomfortable, and I felt that they were annoyed with me. I dreaded that there wasn't enough time. I could not meet their expectations, which were not even mine, and with this realization came a heavy feeling of guilt: *I'm not enough. I should be different. I need to try harder. They are judging me. I must improve myself... Aaaaah! How can I escape? Where is the Exit sign?*

The house of suffering is built on unfulfilled expectations, unmet wants and desires.

All searches for freedom are built on the expectation that says, *Once we get "there," life is going to be so light and easy, so rosy and blissful, that we will be happy forever and ever.* Seeking is based on the expectation of finding lasting happiness by trying to fix something that is not as it should be. Resistance stops as expectations drop and openness is noticed. Seeking and expectation are one process driven by the belief that something needs to happen in order to be content and happy now. One could live in a paradise and not notice if the mind is busy creating *I can't wait for this to happen* scenarios, constantly dreaming about something else.

A spring cleaning of the head to remove all of those useless expectations is the only thing that needs to happen. It's really simple: notice expectations as they arise and see how they hold an image of how it should be in contrast to *how it is*. Feel the gap. See where they come from—your mother, family, partner, kids, boss, community, bank manager. Are these expectations really yours? Do you have to meet these expectations? What happens if you don't? Notice the tension that is connected to the wanting. Feel the sensation. What is *that*?

Of course, the tension is here because of the fear that expectations won't be met. The feelings of sadness, regret, shame, guilt, blame, anger, desperation, and hopelessness, perhaps a wish to die, are all close friends of expectation. If one can let go of wants, shoulds, and should nots, triggers are released too. No more expectations, no more fear that they won't be met, no more resistance to what is here now. In the end, all that is left is surrender.

The mother of all expectations is hope. It's one glorified expectation that tomorrow will be better than today. Hope is a thought about the future that gives birth to expectations. Hope is something that humans have and, yes, it's very nice to see wishes and hopes come true in stories and movies—The Happy Ending. But have a closer look: the more you hope, the less you see what is here and now that can be appreciated right this moment. Letting go of hope is not really about practicing appreciation, but rather a noticing of what is already here, which opens the door for *what is happening* to flow freely. *Ahh!* It feels so good just to be! The smile breaks out and the joy tickles. *Ahh!* That feeling. And one more thing: the flow is a never-ending continuity right here, right now. Being *aware* does not get switched on and off; however, the content is ever changing, like a kaleidoscope of a multicolor experience. In other words, *this* that is happening now is impermanent. Appreciate *this* now, because this, too, shall pass.

Expectations are like clouds that cover the sunshine of *living this moment fully*. If you expect that you should no longer feel unwanted emotions, it is like you are saying no to these feelings when they come up and no to experiencing them fully. Feeling all emotions is the same as having the freedom to live life fully; to experience whatever presents itself, without thinking that it should be different, is priceless. *Freedom* to experience, to feel, to express, to love is already here. Just look behind the curtain of expectations. Don't expect to see only the happy side, because that expectation, too, is a prison. The rich fullness includes all.

Try This for Yourself   Write all this down. When you write, the mind focuses and is forced to look closer.

What do you expect from...?

What do you *not* expect from...?

What do you want from...?

What do you *not* want from...?

Dig deeper and find the hidden expectations.

Write them down, too.

Open up with complete honesty.

When you think that all expectations have been brought up... look for some more.

Write them down.

Read what you have written and let it all sink in.

Let it all be okay.

Acknowledge that these expectations are running in the system.

Take a look in your experience right now. Is anything really missing?

Realize that life goes on regardless of how you expected it to go.

Check whether you have control over what is happening and when.

How about now?

Does *this* care about what you want *this* to be?

See if you need all those expectations or if it's okay to let them all go.

Take a closer look to see if expectations are useful in a practical sense.

See if anything would be lost if those expectations were dropped.

Which expectations would be hardest to let go of?

What are you really looking for? Write all that comes up.

And if this exercise does not have the expected effect, you may bring your precious expectations to the Liberation Unleashed forum and work through them with someone until there is shiny clarity.

Just like weeds in the garden, sneaky expectations may come back. Don't let them ruin the show.

Fear Is Sensation

Fear informs us about itself through an intense sensation. There is a distinct flush that gets triggered by thought, sound, color, smell, taste, or touch. Fear makes itself known as a sudden contraction. It's not pleasant and may set off a chain of reactions. It's felt as a strong *no* to whatever is triggering it.

Imagine for a second that you are in a desert, a wide-open space. You are walking for hours, in circles. You go up yet another hill and see a closed door. It is standing right there, very obvious, and it is locked. There's no key around. No key in your pockets. The door does not move, does not open; it just stands there. You are stunned and cannot move forward. So you sit by the door, and sit some more, thinking, guessing, and dreading what might be behind it. It feels as if the door is guarding something, something that you need but cannot see. At the same time the lock is having a laugh; it has done it's trick, making it appear that there is something important behind the door that is protected. There is another way to find out what is behind the door. No need to unlock it, no need to push it open, just take a step to the side and look behind that silly door. There is nothing there! The desert continues in all directions, and the door stands there, but it's not an obstacle to your journey.

Fear feels and acts like that lock on the door. It stops one from going further. Fear is a signal to step back; it's a warning of danger, real or imagined. The feeling can be so strong that it may paralyze thinking and acting.

Fear is a sensation. It is not to be avoided but rather noticed and felt. It is not good or bad in and of itself. It is doing its job, keeping the self-image and belief structure safe and intact. It's protecting the

I Virus from being found out. At the center of the belief castle is a special belief: *you* as a separate human being, a perceiver of life, in charge of your own choices.

There are many techniques and ways to deal with fear, but let's try something different.

Try This for Yourself Acknowledge the presence of fear when it shows up.

Remain aware that fear is here.

Thank it. Thank it for coming.

Just let it be here for a minute, and see that it's okay for it to be here. Bow to it in honor.

Then look behind it.

What is there? Is anything showing up?

If something does, what is behind that?

Just like that locked door in the desert, you can look from the other side. All you need to do is take a peek, out of curiosity, and see what is there behind that door.

You don't need to go into feeling, nor do you need to analyze the fear endlessly; instead, look at what is hiding behind that sensation of fear. If you feel fear, acknowledge it; if you don't feel it, then don't look for it. There really is nothing to be afraid of.

If the fear is too big, there are ways to reduce it. I recommend the emotional freedom technique (EFT) or whatever works for you. Some people experience a lot of fear during the EFT process, whereas some experience none at all. There is no rule.

Questioning core beliefs does not destroy anything real. Only the false falls away, the false that distorts the view—that holds tension, anxiety, and suffering. The false falling away may feel like a loss, but nothing worth keeping gets lost.

In other words, nothing stops being what it already is. Beliefs that no longer serve are no longer needed, and it's okay to move past them and explore with fresh eyes.

Bypassing fear, making friends with it, using it as a radar to find places of old conditioning that still need cleaning up, are different ways to relate to fear. In these ways, fear can be appreciated. After all, it has been doing such a great job so far.

So take a peek, look behind the fear. What is there that feels threatened? You may find one of two things: nothing at all or something that wants to be seen. Keep looking to see what is there.

When the mind sees that there is nothing behind the fear, the protection mechanism stops protecting that nothing. This may come like a shock, but what is the worst thing that can happen to nothing?

Fear is a friend, really. It is protection. It guards from harm. But all those ideas that appear important cannot be harmed. The image of *me* is made by the mind. It is not something that can be harmed, can disappear, can die, or can be lost; it's an image created by the mind and protected by fear, as if the mind instructed itself to forget to question the self-made image of identity.

Don't fear the sensation of fear. Say yes to it the next time it comes up and see what else you notice about this mechanism, about the nature of sensation and what triggers it. Explore it with curiosity, fearlessly.

Nona

Nona was in a rush when we met in a Facebook group. She was ripe and ready for that recognition. Engaging through Facebook was a rare event for me because I usually communicate through the Liberation Unleashed forum or e-mail, mediums in which the pace is slow, like playing chess. With Nona it was different. We spent only a couple of hours talking directly, and she was as ready for change as people get. I went to sleep after we talked, and in the morning I found her laughing out loud. She got the cosmic joke, and she laughed for three days. It was the simple distinction between thinking and looking that got her to look. I still smile when I remember our chat, which happened four years ago.

Nona became a great guide and is one of the dedicated administrators who look after Liberation Unleashed on a day-to-day basis. She is still as passionate as she was on that first day we met. A real gem.

Ilona: Hi Nona, what brings you here?

Nona: I want to experience no self. Outside of my dreams, I mean.

Ilona: Okay, what do you imagine it is like, what do you expect?

Nona: I imagine it is effortless, similar to the way I experience myself in my dreams. Flowing effortlessly.

Ilona: It already is. Effortless. Only one thing is in the way—belief that it is not.

Nona: Yes. I understand that, and I notice that understanding is not the same as living it.

Ilona: Yes, exactly. So is there a "you" living it?

Nona: Yes, it appears so, and I can't be absolutely sure about that.

Ilona: Aha! So what is it that the word "me" is pointing to?

Nona: A set of beliefs, memories, and a desire for some control over what is experienced. I can question the beliefs and memories, but the desire for control seems implacable.

Ilona: No, no, it points to other thoughts about "me." Check it.

Nona: Yes. They are all thoughts about me.

Ilona: Right, so what is that "me," if not just a thought?

Nona: "Me" is only a belief, and it is a very persistent one. It is my most frequent thought.

Ilona: It's not a belief, it's just a word that is assumed for an entity. Tell me, where do thoughts come from?

Nona: I don't know. They just appear.

Ilona: Take a good look, as well as tell me, can you control thoughts at all?

Nona: I can't find where thoughts come from, and I am not in control of them.

Ilona: So would you say that the thought "me" is appearing by itself?

Nona: I don't know where it comes from. It feels "located" in Nona. Yet I've watched Nona stop being a familiar body and become a ship or a car, exactly identified as the body I feel I currently inhabit.

Ilona: It's simpler than that, really. Tell me, what is Nona?

Nona: Energy. A collection of electrons.

Ilona: No, it's not. It's a character in a story. Can you see Nona as a main character, like Batman, in a fictional story *about* Nona?

Nona: Yes, I can, yes. It's all story. Apparently "my" story.

Ilona: Is there an actor playing a role of Nona?

Nona: No.

Ilona: Aha! So how does a character operate? Is there anything that controls the story?

Nona: What a great question! I'm looking.

Ilona: I'll give you a clue, look at Nona as an organic computer that responds to environment.

Nona: Are you saying that environment creates the story of Nona?

Ilona: Environment greatly influences the story, and shapes it, yes, but is there anything that creates it from outside, like a manager that chooses what happens in the story, that controls events?

Nona: I feel like I almost understand something, but am so dense! The story of Nona appears to be a joint creation between me, my parental units, family, schoolmates. It seems to be added to or impacted on, by all the other stories around this one. The only one choosing what happens in the story of Nona is Nona.

Ilona: It's the same as saying Batman is choosing what he is going to do next in the story of Batman. Choice is also part of story, and the story is fictional. Take a look at Nona from the point of view of a friend, family member, somebody you never met, a colleague: What can you see?

Nona: I see another story of Nona. Nona as a character in my (the friend's) story.

Ilona: Is it the same story or just a story about the same character?

Nona: All our stories are fictional. That's what stories are.

Ilona: Yes. So if I tell you there is no "you" at all, in real life, none as in zero, what comes up right now?

Nona: Neither. My story and your story will be different. Thus the character we call Nona will appear different to each of us. I understand that is true and I notice I don't then let go of the idea that there is a "me." I "get" it; but I don't live it. I ask, then who is typing Nona's part of the conversation? Is this a conversation Ilona is having with herself?

Ilona: There is no "I" to get it—that's the fun part. Notice as it is happening and tell me.

Nona: I feel stupid.

Ilona: Look right at the experience as it is. Right now. Tell me what is happening?

Nona: My story of Ilona is conversing with my story of Nona? Someone is typing. Words are appearing on a screen. That is all.

Ilona: None of that. What do you see right now in front of your eyes? Go in deeper into experience. How does it happen?

Nona: I make it up as I go along.

Ilona: Notice. First reading happens, then thought arises as a response, and fingers start to type.

Nona: Nona is experiencing a story of inquiry.

Ilona: Let's leave Nona for a while and see what is behind the story.

Nona: Okay.

Ilona: What is here now, when you stop thinking about it?

Nona: Breath.

Ilona: Good, good. So look at the breath and see if there is a breather. Do you do the breathing of breath or is it happening by itself?

Nona: Breathing happens by itself.

Ilona: See how language is made: I breathe. I sleep, I walk, I eat. Is there an "I" that does all that?

Nona: No. I am breathed, I am slept. I am walked; it happens and I take credit for it. I incorporate those activities into my story. Much like in my dream, I incorporate noises.

Ilona: Okay, how about dropping that "I" completely: breathing happens, walking happens, taking credit happens.

Nona: Okay. "I" is another piece of language.

Ilona: Is there a doer? Notice as you type the message, notice that it is all happening simultaneously and effortlessly.

Nona: Yes, I see that.

Ilona: Is there an "I" that sees that?

Nona: Understanding happens, and yet there is a persistent sense that understanding is located in a self.

Ilona: That is not a sense, just a thought about it. "Self" is a word.

Nona: It's all just words. All the parts of my stories are words.

Ilona: Take a look. Focus on "I am feeling"—that open, alive, receptive be-ing. See if it's personal. See if it needs to be labeled to feel real.

Nona: I name my experiences. No. It's not personal. And the labels are only to have a way to communicate about it, which may not be necessary either.

Ilona: Observe the mind as a labeling machine. Look around the room and notice things, see how thoughts label everything automatically.

Nona: Yes.

Ilona: Is there anything that does not happen on automatic?

Nona: No.

Ilona: Do you exist?

Nona: Only as a character in a story.

Ilona: Okay, but do you exist in reality? The story is fiction.

Nona: And yet this character has a sense of self, labels about a self.

Ilona: Let's see, does Batman exist? Does a unicorn exist? Does the tooth fairy exist?

Nona: No. Those are also fictions. If Nona does not exist in reality, where are these experiences she's telling herself?

Ilona: Let's go back to the sense of self. Take a look. What is it? Is it self or aliveness plus a label?

Nona: Aliveness plus a label.

Ilona: Now look at experience. Is there an experiencer?

Nona: No, and the story of Nona is a story of experiences, neatly labeled.

Ilona: Check it—look at experience now, really close. What is behind experience?

Nona: Thought.

Ilona: No, not thought. Thought comes later. Take a look again.

Nona: Sensation.

Ilona: Behind sensation, is there anything that sensation is happening to?

Nona: Something believes it is having sensation, and that's a thought. Nona doesn't seem to be getting this.

Ilona: What is that something?

Nona: I don't know.

Ilona: Take a look.

Nona: Aliveness?

Ilona: Let this settle today. We can talk more tomorrow. Focus on experience, on now, notice how thoughts are also part of experience.

Nona: Thank you.

Ilona: You are welcome.

The next day on Facebook…

Nona: Great belly-laughs! It has constructed an elaborate story of a guide at a gate in order to explain no self to the character Nona. As if Nona existed. Direct experience of feet on tile floor; direct experience of hands in water; reports (thoughts) about washing dishes. No Nona needed.

How amazing to go from a belief that Nona is a character in a story to observing the story being built *while it looks*. Hilarious! The story gets a chapter about a search for a Nona, complete with explanations and reports concerning its makeup and status. The story has

Nona running around looking for no self and not finding it. Ha ha ha ha ha!

Elena: Welcome home, honey. ;)

Nona: Still laughing!

Elena: Ha ha ha ha ha—laughing with you! Ha ha ha! This is really hilarious, to search all life to find this, yes. :) All of this life is for the sake of seeking self, but there is no self out there...

Nona: The simplicity of it. Yes! Ha ha ha ha ha! Ilona said *look*; not *think*. D'oh! Ha ha ha ha ha! *Looking* is amazing. There's no Nona in *looking*.

Elena: Yay, honey. Much love.

Nona: Ilona, *thank you so much!*

Ilona: You are very welcome! Live free, love. How is life feeling today?

Nona: Fantastic! Nothing has changed; everything appears different.

Still Laughing! :-D

Ilona: It's a cosmic joke! :)

Nona: Can't believe it's only day two! I noticed the physical sensations of anger coming up today; but there was no self for it to catch on to and the feelings disappeared. Not at all business as usual for this one!

A couple of days passed and more people came in to the conversation to congratulate Nona...

Jeff: Hi Nona, Congrats on discovering the grand illusion. Happy looking! ;-)

Lisa: Yay, Nona!

Nona: Day three: awaiting developments. Noticing effortlessness where "I" used to snag on thoughts and emotions as they arose. Thoughts and feelings still arise; no assistance or interference from Nona is needed. Not feeling disconnected; on the contrary, feeling quite connected. Now what?

Lisa: Still laughing?

Nona: Oh yes! It's still so hilarious! Looking and laughing here!

Lisa: Well big fat happy "yay" to that!

Three years later I asked Nona for an update, and here is what she wrote.

Nona: What changed for me?

I suddenly noticed that *everything* that was happening in my world was truly, genuinely, completely okay, regardless of what thoughts said. It was a lie that I had ever been a "me" in control of "my" life. I actually laughed for three straight days over that!

What were the challenges?

The biggest challenge was not believing that I should somehow now be completely free from stressful thoughts; that without a belief in a "me" as creator of my world, conditioned thoughts and behaviors would simply all drop away.

Habit persists, despite having seen through the illusion of a separate self, and continuing to notice that thought tells stories that may not be supported by direct experience is very important. Checking direct experience for proof of what thoughts say has been a most useful practice.

The key for me to living rooted in the realization of no separate self was knowing that "no self" is not a *state* that can pass; it's not a way of being or of thinking or feeling, but a plain fact just like "no Santa." We don't expect to "abide in no Santa"; we simply know that Santa is not an entity in reality once we've discovered that.

What advice can I offer?

Return to the uninterpreted moment; your truth is there, before the stories. That's where quiet and peace can invariably be found. All it takes is a shift of focus.

Recognition

Once it's seen, it cannot be unseen. This statement refers to recognition. In other words, what is recognized will always be recognized, no matter the situation (unless, of course, you have memory problems).

Let's say you meet someone and ten years later you meet her again—instant recognition happens. It's underneath the thinking. Recognition is something that operates outside of thoughts. You meet that old friend and recognize her simply because she has a unique face, body structure, voice, and so forth. It's like learning the colors in childhood; a child is shown the color and is told that it is called "red." That child then recognizes red at any time in life as being "red." You hear a song once, and the second time you recognize it—*I've heard that song before.*

When we look at something familiar, recognition takes place—the "aha!" moment. We don't need to philosophize or make logical connections to simply recognize what is already the case.

It's difficult to see the illusion of a separate self only because it has never occurred to us to deeply question the assumptions, *I am a separate entity, I have an identity.* The "I-thought" is assumed to be "me," the doer and thinker, a subject with free will and choice. When we start digging into these assumptions, it becomes obvious that an "I-entity" cannot be found. When you face this head-on, recognition happens. "There is no separate self" can just be words that raise your eyebrows, or they can be a knowing that is beyond thought.

What is, simply is, without any manager, orchestrator, or puppet master pulling strings. Life is just happening, and everything is happening within it, as *it*. Nothing is separate from anything else. Everything is dependent upon everything else as one movement, one dance—empty and yet so rich in its fullness.

Recognition is a moment when we know that we know. It's something familiar showing up; it may have been forgotten, or it may have been denied, but once that recognition happens, it is not possible to unrecognize that pattern. Once the seeing happens, once it becomes clear that the separate self is an illusion, it can never be truly forgotten again. Different situations arise with different levels of intensity, but what has been seen can be seen over and over and over again in every situation. It's not hidden. When we look at what is obvious, without thinking or referring to a memory, without trying to fit it into models of reality or to match it to the descriptions given by teachers, there is an intimate, instant recognition. *This is.* This is what is happening now; the rest is a story.

No one can convince you that you recognize something. Of course you can pretend and say that you do and make logical explanations, express opinions, have debates, write books, and teach about it. But deep knowing comes from within, from looking for yourself, from wanting to know beyond doubt.

It's funny how we can stare at the wall of an imaginary prison, feeling stuck, waiting to transcend it, and not recognize that there is no prison, that the wall is imagined. We believe all kinds of stories and try to escape this feeling by resisting, denying, expecting something else, and getting lost in fearful thoughts. All that is needed is recognition—there is nothing here that is bound and limited. There is no prisoner trying to escape; it's all just a habitual, dull, and painful story in the head.

When we recognize a story to be just a story and not reality, the glue that holds us stuck in the story suddenly starts dissolving. We no longer believe the story is "the truth of how things are." We recognize it as a description, an interpretation, or an entertaining thought. It becomes easier to step back and notice that there is something else going on besides the thought-story; it becomes possible to notice peace underneath all thoughts.

This, which is happening right now, is not bound to a story; it just *is*. If a story arises, it is seen as part of *what is*, within it. Not the driver, not the separate self—just a thought-story about what is happening. Along with the sense perceptions and feelings, it's happening *as* thoughts. A sense of self can arise, no problem with that, but it's also recognized as something that arises and passes away, like all phenomena. The sense of self is no longer seen as something solid, permanent, or existing in and of itself. Sense of self is seen as sensation, a feeling, not the experiencer.

Recognition is not intellectual, philosophical, or a matter of logic. It does not involve thought. It is awareness that something is true, a click when something fits. Like déjà vu, recognition is a sense that this has happened before. Recognition is a click—the aha point, that's what we are talking about. It's a moment of cognition about something that we already know. When the last piece of the puzzle falls into place, the image is suddenly finished; it no longer seems to be made of parts, rather you see it as a whole picture.

You may think that this recognition comes as a grand awakening experience, but it can be so subtle, nearly unnoticeable at first, until you start to notice the implications. So don't look for a big bang that may or may not happen. Recognition is not a special elevated state. Don't wait for a special feeling, because recognition may be pretty ordinary and pass unnoticed.

At Liberation Unleashed we use the term "Gateless Gate," borrowed from Zen tradition, to describe a Gate that does not exist; there is literally nothing in the way to the here and now, but for a spiritual seeker there appears to be a solid wall that needs to be broken through in order to find the happy ever after. Crossing the Gateless Gate is an opening to further exploration; it's not a "done" point but rather the single-most important recognition of emptiness, after which life is no longer the same. It's not just the end of another chapter in life's journey, it's the end of a book. Then a new book starts.

When a child recognizes that Santa was never real, a belief about the magical superbeing falls away; the child gets that the mystery of presents is no longer a mystery but a belief in a fairy tale—no more than that. The child can no longer believe in Santa; no matter how convincing the parents may be, the child knows it was a trick. It may be a disappointing, shattering event, but even then Christmas and presents can still be enjoyed, the game can still be played, but no one gets fooled by it anymore. Now the child can tell other kids about this realization and, in turn, the little believers-in-magic can see the truth of Santa. It does not mean that "no Santa" replaces Santa. The bubble bursts with a silent pop. That's all.

Sacha

What follows is a conversation I had on the Ruthless Truth forum in 2011. It was the first conversation I had on a forum with anyone. For me it started the journey of Direct Pointing and Liberation Unleashed. This was a little spark that ignited the fire that excited me enough to carry on, to share, and to sound the wake-up call louder. Sacha was great; our chat happened over two days, and on the third day he saw. He was as ready to look as it gets and was relentless. Soon after this conversation, Sacha started to point, and he became a great guide; a dedicated, key member of Liberation Unleashed; and a beautiful friend.

Ilona: I'll help with all I got, just bring yourself to me; let's examine this together.

Sacha: The last few days have been quite interesting. Examining, for the first time really, the notion and experience of self, of me. I'm a bit puzzled by the fact that the assumption of self has been left unscrutinized for so many years and amazed by the ease with which any notion of self is dissolved by asking if that notion is really true.

So you asked me to bring myself to you for further examination. Problem is, I can't really find a self when looking for it. Yet, something seems to be holding me back, as if I cannot really accept the fact that there might actually be no one there.

I would describe the place I'm at as clinging to a very vague, yet very intimate and familiar "sense of self."

Ilona: Hi Sacha! Let's see.

The sense of being is the same as it has always been and always will be. That is the basic "I am" awareness. That is the only true thing that I know. I am.

Let this be and have a look at the individual self. You say that you cannot find it. Describe what it is you find when looking for the self. What is holding you back is fear—the fear that there is no you. Can you examine the fear? See if you notice what it is protecting.

If there is no one here, then no one needs protection, right?

Now look at life through the lens of no self and see what you notice. Does life need a manager in a form of you?

Or is it happening all by itself?

Sacha: I can find nothing (real) at all, that's the silly thing about this. The question I've been asking myself is, *What is meant when I say "I"?* Not the body, not the mind, not the totality of body-mind, not the brain, nor a special organ in the brain. These are obviously not what I refer to when I say "I." So then, less physical notions of self appear: an incorporeal ghost inhabiting this body (a soul of sorts) and so forth. But these kinds of ideas are highly speculative and really don't make any sense at all.

So I understand that what I call the self is really nothing more than an idea, or a cluster of ideas that have reality only in the domain of thought.

What is holding you back is fear—the fear that there is no you. Can you examine the fear? See if you notice what it is protecting.

You are right about the fear that comes up in this process. This fear is felt very distinctly as a physical sensation, as if a knot is being tightened in the area of the stomach. A nauseating and overwhelming feeling. What is it protecting? I guess a sense of "being in control"—no, I'm sure of it actually—the tightness is attempting to create a barrier between a weak, scared, fragile self that wants to keep the other at a safe distance. There is fear of being seen naked, of being vulnerable to criticism, ridicule, of "being found out." Funny thing, come to think of it, is that this fear has always been the fear of being found out as a fraud. I've never really understood where this fear came from, but it is beginning to make some more sense now.

At this particular moment, the fear mainly revolves around the control issue. Afraid to relinquish control, afraid of becoming a vegetable, a zombie, of not being able to take care of myself and family.

If there is no one here, then no one needs protection, right?

That makes sense. It is not experienced as such, however.

Now look at life through the lens of no self and see what you notice. Does life need a manager in a form of you?

Or is it happening all by itself?

I can see how ridiculous the notion of a me controlling life is—but the reluctance and resistance to really consider the idea that there has never been nor ever will be an individual self is pretty strong. This creates tension, because the longing for the truth of this is getting more intense by the day.

Thanks for taking the time to examine this with me.

Ilona: Thank you for answering with honesty and taking the time to examine it.

Let's deal with the fear first. It is a very understandable fear of not being in control. It is scary to let go, of course. But fear is here for a reason—protection. Can you honor that fear? Just look at it as a powerful mechanism and honor it. It does its job. It's okay. You can let it go. You have never been in control. It's easy to let go when you see that there has never been an option to control *what is*.

Fear of being caught as a fraud—right on. Self is a fraud; the mind pretended it was real and forgot that it wasn't!

Resistance is also part of a mechanism in the system that protects imaginary self from harm. Only in the mind.

Life was never given to us, we can never own it, simply because life expresses as us before we express as life. Not two. The life force that moves an animal is the same life force that moves plants and human bodies. Somehow there grows an assumption that it is the "I" that is the one that moves and thinks. It is in the system until examined and seen for being the fraud that it is—the core fraud upon which beliefs build a castle for ego and which sets in motion all kinds of protection.

Truth is simple—life *is*.

If truth is all you want—look, it's in front of your eyes! There is no separate life force that moves the separate body. There is no thinker, no watcher, but experience happening. Now.

Now look at the idea that there really is no you; it's okay, whatever fear comes up, acknowledge, honor, and let go.

Look closer. Is it possible? Is it true?

Sacha: I want to look a little bit closer at this fear. You say that it is there for a reason and that it does its job. Its job of what: Of protecting something that doesn't exist at all? That seems strange.

I can see that what is trying to hide behind these walls is nothing substantial at all, but what I do not understand is how, where, when, and why this mistake was made in the first place. Why is this organism fighting to protect something that does not exist? Perhaps it doesn't really matter and this is another distraction that keeps me from really looking at this.

I feel a little bit stuck at the moment. You tell me to look more closely at the idea that there is no me. You ask: Is it true?

I understand that it must be—still, I do not really see how it could be so.

Ilona: You don't need to know and understand everything about the wall in order to demolish it. Just look at what it is inside that resists the idea that there is no you.

Locate the idea, look at it, and see it for what it is—a belief planted in a mind in a form of thought.

There is no "you" that is separate from life. The idea of separation is just a belief.

How would the world look without this belief?

Observe and notice what comes up.

Sacha: Well, it would mean the end of struggling, grasping, trying to understand, defending, and attacking. The end of desperately trying to control each and every detail of a situation in order to prevent me from feeling bad about myself. It would mean the end of avoiding situations that could possibly lead to "me being found out as a fraud."

If there is no me, if that me has always been only a thought, then that would mean freedom, for sure. Life would just be as it is, it would be accepted without conditions. *Oh, I will only show myself if such-and-such conditions are there in order for me to feel safe and secure.* It would mean that the searching for a "true self" or "higher self" (whatever that means) would make no sense at all. Dealing with life would not be postponed until an ideal situation has been actualized.

Life would just be lived, I guess. Not suffered by a separated being.

I can see that, Ilona, and I feel the truth of it. It seems as if I just have to muster up the courage to jump into the truth of it.

Earlier this morning, having breakfast with my son, playing with him, bathing him, and even now sitting here typing these words, I cannot find a separate self that is doing it, an entity making choices and deciding what actions are taken. There is no effort in any of this. What does still remain, however, is this nagging sense of being stuck somewhere, of holding back.

Although looking at this knot, right now, at the tightness and the constriction of it, already seems to loosen it. Instead of feeling hard and immovable, it can be felt as warmth. I'll sit with this for a while.

You have some more ideas on how to let this go?

Ilona: Trust that all you know about life is not what it is.

Then just look.

What is going on?

I can see that the knot is loosening. Good. Now step forward. No "you"—there never was. See it. Let the seeing happen. There really is no you to let it happen. Just watch it unfold.

Sacha: Okay. I can let the fear go by just letting it be as it is. It is fully experienced, seen to have no actual content, and then it dissolves. That's great and I thank you for looking at this with me, but that's not really important, is it?

What remains is a very quiet mind and a sensation of being detached. I cannot keep the eyes open, so they close. There is the distinct experience of the space of awareness growing larger and larger. Thoughts arise, but there is no one creating them, they simply emerge, triggered by a sound, a sensation, whatever. The senses receive information and it is registered, sometimes leading to associations or memories.

Any action taken either just happens spontaneously or is preceded by a thought. The sense of expansion and detachment is striking, really, but it is still exactly that: the experience of observing phenomena.

It's as if I'm waiting for some dramatic falling away of this sense of separation. Does that make sense to you?

Ilona: There won't be dramatic change, no angelic trumpets, and no bright lights in the eyes. The shift is very subtle. It may be that looking back you won't even know when it really happened.

You are seeing it already, just the mind says no; it's like being used to one thing and expecting that to change.

With your eyes closed, is there a feeling of separation? Focus on that for a while—give yourself space to do this.

When the eyes are open all mental processes kick in and labeling starts. It's just thoughts registering what's going on. But you don't need to believe thoughts anymore!

Just relax for a bit and forget everything. Take a break, if possible get out in nature; outside, watch the body breathing and notice that it breathes with and without a watcher.

Report what you find.

Sacha: Excellent idea! Could really use some extra oxygen at this point.

I'll report back later.

Later…

What to say?

Something has shifted completely this afternoon. I can honestly say that the self, my self, does not exist, has never existed. It has always been nothing more than a thought, an imagined journey to an imagined goal that was bound for utter failure.

As a matter of fact, life happens quite successfully without someone living it.

So no halo or wings? Or is that the next level? Where do I sign up for that? ;)

There's still a bit of a rush and an elevated heart rhythm as these words appear—it's quite amazing how vibrant and alive everything is now. The body is literally shaking with energy. The perceptual shift that has occurred is indeed quite simple and subtle, but it cannot be missed. The fact that there is no self is very, very visible. There is just this, experience, no individual being experiencing it, judging it, trying to influence it in any way. How could that be possible?

The sense of self is still there, as are all memories, thoughts. Everything is exactly as it was. There is just a clear seeing of the fact that there is no me involved in all of this.

Had to lie down for a bit as waves and waves of heat flushed through the body. Feverish almost. What is this?

I think it's a good idea to let this settle for a bit. Any feedback on this?

Ilona: Seems like you opened your eyes for the first time. :)

Relax, rest, and let it settle…and then write a big post about what you see. Explore a bit further, see with new eyes, share what you see.

Yeah, no trumpets, but it's way better than that!

Sacha: I'm happy to announce that I have not turned into a vegetable.

Also, I have not suddenly gained supernatural powers. I would like to speak to the management about this.

Kidding aside, I understand that it is customary for newly liberated people to write up a big post about their experiences. I'll give it my best shot.

It is difficult to pinpoint "the shift" to a particular moment. In retrospect it is more like a process that took a couple of days, a process of a misconception—"there is a (real) self"—being seen for *what is*. Reading some of the material on this forum, some of the associated blogs, and really taking time to seriously examine the notion of self was a very helpful preparation for the letting go. And it is quite simple, really. What is asked is to simply, quietly, and without interruption look at all the assumptions, beliefs, and conceptions of the idea of "you," the one living your life, the sailor that steers your boat on the ocean of existence, so to speak.

Looking at this, really looking at this question, "What is referred to when I speak/think of 'me,'" is a big taboo. It is seen as either a pubescent attempt to find one's place in the world or a deluded question asked by people with mental problems, or new age softies. It is considered to be self-evident and in no need of further scrutiny.

Well, it is [in need of scrutiny]. There is nothing there. Absolutely nothing. Never has been and never will. Void, emptiness, nothing at all. Just a messy knot of unchecked assumptions, memories, and a dramatic story that wouldn't look out of place in a soap opera.

I understand a lot more of the way that language has been used here on Ruthless Truth in order to point to the truth of this, that there truly is no self, especially the harsh language. You somehow have to get the full attention of that which people call "themselves." I guess that for a lot of people, anger, defensiveness, and a sense of being attacked is the right trigger to get this self-idea clearly in the picture. Then that can be examined and shown to be wholly fictional.

For me, the trigger was fear. As I posted earlier, it was a deep-rooted fear of losing control, of "turning into a vegetable" and not being able to take care of myself and my loved ones. A very real, visceral fear that was experienced very tangibly around the stomach. A very familiar fear. Ilona gently guided me to really look at this fear. What was it protecting?

At this point, something interesting happened. The eyes closed and the feeling of fear became clearer and more pronounced. All that was done was looking, simple looking. No effort, no straining, nothing. The tightness of the fear released and what remained was warmth, radiating outwards. It was clearly seen that the "self" that was thought to be protected, shielded from an apparently hostile world, was not there. There was literally nothing to be protected.

What really did the trick for me was Ilona's emphasis on acknowledging this fear for what is—not trying to negate it, run away from it, or any such thing—just looking it straight in the eye. What is it trying to protect?

I can see that the knot is loosening. Good. Now step forward. No "you"—there never was. See it. Let the seeing happen. There really is no you to let it happen. Just watch it unfold.

You are seeing it already, just the mind says no; it's like being used to one thing and expecting that to change.

These words pushed me right over the edge. What I needed was a real faith (perhaps "trust" is a better word) that what was being pointed to is really, actually the case. There was an instant of not knowing anything, not doing anything, and then the belief in self fell away completely.

Quite a bit of physical phenomena came up with that, as the knot of self untangled. Very intense waves of heat were felt throughout the body. Even now, the senses relay information much more intensely. It is as if reality, experience, is seen in its complete vibrant aliveness. There is no one experiencing it, seeing it through layers and layers of assumptions, fears, and so forth. Much more direct.

Where there was the knot in the stomach there is now quiet emptiness, nothing.

For the rest, nothing much has changed, really. I had the idea that seeing through the illusion of self would be a dramatic moment, a great achievement with the audience gasping in excitement. No such thing—all that happens is that the story of self is seen for what it is: a story, a work of fiction. This it has always been. It simply was left unchecked and taken for granted.

It's funny to realize that there has never actually been a self behind it all—that it was simply the one great unchecked assumption that just needed one honest glance to dissolve. That is really all it takes, just one instant of really seeing it for what it is.

Experience now is pretty much the same as it was earlier, exactly the same: simply ordinary, everyday existence with assorted thoughts and feelings. The only small difference is that it is now no longer assumed that there is anyone experiencing it, there is just this experience.

That's all I've got at this moment.

I really want to express deep gratitude to you for the gentle pointing and giving me that final push.

Ilona: I'm delighted for you! Welcome to the new way of being— glad to be of service and I hope soon you can start helping others here.

Much love.

Sacha: Thanks again for stepping into the story of me for a moment and blowing it up from the inside! I like how no harshness of words was needed for this.

There's still some shakiness here, as if the body is readjusting to this, but I'm sure it will settle.

All love, S.

Ilona: Nice work Sacha, you are very welcome!

There was no need for harshness since you have been honest and did not try to fool yourself or others. I also know that gentleness is power.

Can we be friends on Facebook? Find me through my blog.

Sacha: I'd love to but I don't have a Facebook account anymore and no plans of reactivating it anytime soon.

We'll keep in touch one way or another.

I asked Sacha to write a couple of words for the book; this was in November 2014.

Reading back the conversation I had with Ilona in June 2011, what comes up first is a deep gratitude. Ilona's guiding came exactly at the right time. Like a lot of us, I had been searching for answers, for peace and happiness, for well over a decade, mostly seeking refuge in spirituality, academia, and altered states. A never-ending and ultimately frustrating going in circles. Then, seemingly out of the blue, the question *What is the self?* arose and lit a fire that burned everything. Ilona was the perfect guide for me, urging me to keep looking and fully allow and accept the deep-rooted fear that this investigation triggered. Then there was an instant that everything fell away, total surrender. Full stop. All energy dropped from the head down into the heart. Life came rushing in and experience changed dramatically. The first couple of days I was unable to function properly, it was as if all filters were completely gone. Experience was raw, direct, and intense. This state lasted for more than a year.

Now things have settled and life continues as always. Big difference: a very quiet mind and a warm heart.

My recommendation to seekers is simple. Find out one thing: The self, what is it? Be relentless in your investigation. Don't settle for any answer. Make finding out the truth about this, once and for all, your absolute top priority. You should be burning with desire to discover what is real and what is not. Keep looking at this from every conceivable angle. Keep looking.

Love, S.

Concepts, Words, and Stories Are Not What They Seem

Language is a tool for communicating. We can share stories with others, ask advice, learn, study, plan, solve problems, create, and explore. We use language every day; we think in words. Language has become so ingrained that we don't look at it directly to see how it works, why it works, or what is behind it. Unless you study language, it is not something that you think much about.

Let's take a closer look: Words are symbols, units of information, carriers of meaning. They are pointers, like fingers that point to objects. Words point to meaning. Our experiences are named by words that mean something to us. When we communicate, we exchange ideas, concepts, and stories that make us feel a certain way. The meaning is perceived and understood, and the feeling gets communicated.

When I say a few words, they land in the listener. The listener takes on board a meaning from those words, so the words are interpreted and seen through filters of beliefs; then the new idea is either confirmed or rejected. The same words can mean different things to different people or different things in different situations. It is not up to the speaker where her words land. Words land where they land and, just like a pebble thrown into a pond, words create ripples in the pool of already accepted ideas.

The meaning of a word is not the word itself but is found within what is meant by the unit of language. It is easy to get stuck on concepts and believe that they are telling the truth, but none of them are truth, they are only carriers. It's easy to look at the finger that points to the moon and assume that the finger itself is where focus should go. If you get hooked on looking at the finger, you can discuss the finger, debate about it, argue about it, and even create a following, but the moon is not there. The moon is located where the finger is pointing to. You can miss and forget the pointing entirely if all you can see is the pointing tool. My cat does this: he always looks at the finger, not where it points.

Ideas are not objects or subjects themselves. Groups of concepts taken for truth of how things are become beliefs upon which new ideas land and stick, creating an even bigger, more magnificent castle of concepts. What seems to be "my world," the totality of my experience of all that is happening, is a creation of language, and words are the building blocks that create the story about it.

All I have are words. You read these words and understanding happens. If the idea is truly understood, you are able to say the same thing in your own words and express the same idea in a different way. This process is like having ten painters painting the same landscape: all of the paintings will be of the same scenery, but different hands with unique expressions create them. My job as a writer is to paint the word picture so that you can recognize the landscape and see what I am talking about in your own experience, even if I use words that are not the ones that you would use. Your job as a reader is to get the meaning *behind* the words.

Words are not experience. The story about experience is not experience. Experience is what is happening through sense perception: seeing, hearing, tasting, smelling, touching, feeling, and thinking. What is happening underneath the words is what the words are pointing to. Taste an apple and see; its sweetness, crunchiness, and juiciness are ideas that are learned, repeated, and accepted as standard expressions. They only vaguely describe what is happening on taste buds. But, if you share that apple with a friend, both of you will know what you mean by these descriptions and agree.

Language creates objects and subjects out of thin air. It creates a doer, someone who does the action; the mover of something. The English language is based on nouns and verbs. Nouns tell us who or what the doer is, whereas verbs describe actions. We have sentences and statements like "The grass is growing," in which the grass *becomes* the doer of growing. Or "I am breathing," in which the "I" seems as though it is the doer that does the breathing, and so on.

The story about experience can be shared, and that in and of itself is an experience. If we focus on concepts and think that they express a solid reality, we get lost in the theory. Being lost in the head can be fun, but most often it is not. Realizing the empty nature of *all* concepts frees the mind. Holding on to ideas creates limitation, boundaries, opinions, differences, and even wars.

"My self" is a concept. That is just the beginning of it. Seeing that there is no actual discrete entity behind the words "my" and "self" opens up the doors to further exploration.

For a day or two, pay attention to language itself. See how ideas are communicated. See how concepts are built on other concepts, which, in turn, are standing on even more concepts, creating one huge bubble in which everything makes sense in the context of the other ideas.

Words themselves do not mean anything until we agree on their meaning—a meaning that is based in experience. If we don't agree about the meaning of a collection of letters and the sound they make, say "gortumack," then they are just a collection of random letters and a sound we can make.

So, it all comes down to these questions: What is it that the letters and the sound "my self" mean? What do they point to? Where do they land?

When the mind sees that all concepts are empty, it no longer needs to focus on thinking so much. Stories about past and future eventually stop playing out. "Shoulds" and "should nots" become less important, and the story becomes transparent. The story does not disappear, but it is seen as empty, not solid, not that serious, and, sometimes, even hilarious. It still appears that there is a "me," but it is known to be a useful concept, not the truth. Then, the mind can relax and come back to it's natural state of being open, curious, joyful, playful, and free. It can notice spaciousness and oneness when it is no longer trying to fit and organize experience into a frame of fixed ideas.

It's not that one belief about how things are is true, while another one isn't. All beliefs are not true—*all* concepts, models, and maps of reality are trying to find ways to explain the inexplicable. When you see that all knowledge is composed of made-up stories, those stories lose their grip. Attention goes to *being* rather than thinking; that is where peace is found. Stories still come up, but they aren't fed attention nor given dramatized exaggeration; they are seen through quickly. Labels are no longer assumed to be "things." Freedom lies in seeing that concepts are creations of language that serve the purpose of communicating. They are practical, but empty.

Ideas Are Hypnotic by Nature

When you get an idea to do something exciting, it's like a lightbulb switching on, and there is this sense of anticipation, fun, and future fulfillment. Ideas become the center of attention around which the rest of the thinking organizes itself. New ideas don't just come and pass by without making a ripple; sometimes there's a big wave or even a tsunami to the system. When ideas become beliefs and are accepted as how things really are, all experience organizes around that, and we perceive the world through the frame of a core structure that is made up of beliefs. The core idea that influences all experience is the idea of separateness, a belief in a separate entity called "me," an assumption that there is an "I" who is observing experience from outside and to which life is happening.

Thoughts may say many things, fantastic and surreal, and steal attention from what is underneath the conceptual overlay. Living, as we do, in the so-called information age, suggestions come from everywhere, affirmation and confirmation are working without taking any time off. Ideas that we feel to be the truth create the basis of our worldview. We get hypnotized by suggestions before we even know it. My aim is to get you to challenge the certainty, the solidity of ideas, to inspire you to unhypnotize yourself and initiate a rebalancing of the core organizing system, to break out of the soft prison of concepts so you can come back to the natural way of being, free of the I Virus.

Thoughts are generally noisy, and they sound important. At the same time, they *are* what is happening. Ideas about life are part of life. It's only that aliveness is not found in ideas; it's found in the spaciousness of being, the subtle sense of "Here I am" before it's expressed verbally. In other words, aliveness is not found in the mind, the mind is found in aliveness.

Concepts are all I have to point you to the places between the thoughts, the silence, the space of being, and the sweetness of being alive. Please don't assume anything; don't take my suggestions as truth, but use them to dig deeper and find that which is hidden underneath them.

Try This for Yourself   Have a piece of fruit handy, or something that you like to eat. Put it aside for now. Get a pen and paper ready.

Start this exercise by imagining that you are holding the fruit. Close your eyes and see the fruit in vivid detail. Then imagine eating the fruit; feel the sensations of taste, texture, and fragrance. Enjoy the imaginary fruit as much as you can. Feel your mouth watering.

Now actually bite the fruit and see the difference between your thoughts and experience; notice how experience is richer. Feel the sensations and experience the fruit with curiosity, as if you have never tasted the fruit before. Feel all as much as you can. Savor it. Take a few bites, enjoy the flavor, and be aware of all sensations.

Now, using pen and paper, describe the experience of taste and smell in as much detail as possible. Write for a couple of minutes about both experiences, comparing the imagined fruit to the real one, describing what was different.

For the final part, compare these three experiences: imaginary fruit, real fruit, and description. What do you notice? Can you bite the words on the paper and experience sensations of taste and smell? Can you see that words don't ever touch the real experience that happens on the taste buds? See how the concepts of sweet, juicy, tasty, and delicious are not the actual sweetness and deliciousness that you experienced but a mere shadow of experience put into words. Concepts are not experience.

The Trick of Language

When we learn to say our first words as children, parents are so happy. We learn fast and start to communicate what we want. We learn to say "I," "me," and "mine," and we understand that these are very important words because we get what we want by using them. It's *my* toy, *my* mum, *I* want this, *I* don't want to share *my* stuff.

Our verbal thoughts appear as words and strings of words joined into sentences.

Language and Labels

Because of the way language is constructed, we have labels for objects and we have labels for actions. Every word is a pointer to something, be it practical or imaginary, but words themselves are only labels, symbols. Nouns like "house," "car," "woman," "cat," "thought," "feeling," and "sun" point to objects, to ideas, to something that appears solid.

Language Assumes a "Doer"

When we express some action through words, there is always an assumed doer of action: *I* breathe, *I* walk, *I* watch TV, *I* hear a sound, *you* listen to the music, *we* are having dinner, *a car* is passing by. There is always someone or something *doing*. But when we look close and try to find that doer, it's nowhere to be found; it's only a construct of language. We assume that "I" is an entity/doer who is supposedly outside of experience.

If language was constructed from verbs only, the world would feel quite different: breathing, typing, looking around, hearing music, talking to a friend, walking, eating...all the action could be expressed without a subject, and it would still be pointing to the same action. If the word "I" is dropped, nothing changes other than the way of describing. (Doing so might make it more difficult to communicate, though, or it would radically change the whole basis of communication.)

But What If There Is No Doer?

I breathe—breathing is happening. See, there is no "I" who is the breather. In actuality there is a sensation of movement of breath, in and out. The word "I" becomes the center point of life, one that needs to be protected, defended, and looked after. Great. But it's only an idea, a label pointing to nothing that can be perceived by senses.

Ilona is typing this. I am typing this. Typing is happening. The same movement can be expressed through different words, but the action itself does not depend on how it's labeled. Instead of using the word "Ilona" to point to this body, it's agreed that the word "I" should be used; it's a convenient word to use in a conversation with you. But neither Ilona, nor I, is doing the typing. Typing is happening effortlessly as the next thought comes up.

Somehow we humans became the victims of language through the assumption of a separate entity. The I/me only creates misery and unnecessary suffering. Some call it "ego." Humans not only learned to speak but also learned to never question this assumption, as everyone around us is trapped in the same invisible prison of words. That I am separate from you is the most common thing to believe, and it's taken for granted.

Remember—language is only a tool.

Labels

When I was a little child, I learned to speak by labeling things, looking from "me" here to what is "other" out there. At least this is how I remember it.

Mum: What is this?

Ilona: This is a house. This is a car. This is a window. This is me.

Mum: Where is your nose?

Ilona: Here is my nose [touching it].

I learned to label things and experiences and tested my limits and the limits of my parents' patience by throwing things, by saying no, and by resisting conditioning. You know that "little rebel" age if you have kids.

I learned language and started using it, communicating with other people. The most important words were "I," "me," "myself," and "mine": this is *my* toy, not my brother's.

This belief in a me as a separate object became strong; it became the central belief around which everything else was happening. Like the belief that Earth is the center of the universe, I became the center of my world inasmuch as my world was filled with my experiences, my things, my knowledge, and my ego...until I looked.

It really was just one look; it took only a few seconds, and the whole search was over. I saw the search for clarity, the quest of *Who am I?*, as a cosmic joke.

There is no "who." There is "am," but no "I." Just "being," a verb. There is no doer of am-ness. There is nothing here in direct experience that is separate from experienced. Just this. Always now.

If you want to test this, simply do this little experiment that won't take much of your time. All you need is twenty minutes, a pen, and paper.

Try This for Yourself   First, write what you are experiencing right now using the words "I," "me," and "my." Get right to the point: don't write about past or future fantasy, just a plain description of here and now.

Like this:

I am lying in bed. I am hearing the rain. I am typing these words. I am feeling cold. I hear the cat's footsteps.

Do this for a full ten minutes. Watch the body. Are there any sensations of tightening or relaxing? Write out all that is happening within these ten minutes in a most descriptive way. Focus on what is happening around you—sounds, sensations, visual experiences—rather than the thinking process.

Then, for the next ten minutes, write without the words "I," "me," and "my." Just describe the experience as it is happening using verbs alone.

Like this:

Waiting for next thought, typing, breathing, blinking. Hearing the rain. Waiting for the next thought. Hearing birds singing.

Again, watch what is happening in the body. Don't just rewrite what you wrote in the first part, rather focus on the here and now and describe what arises as it arises, keeping it always fresh.

Now compare the two ways of labeling the experience. Is one truer than the other? If so, which one? What is here without labels? Do labels affect the experience or just describe it? How did the body react? Which way of describing felt more natural, more relaxing?

Have a look. Does a description affect how you feel about what is described? Can you see that thoughts describe and create a story at the same time? Can you see that the word "I" is part of description and not as important as it seems?

Having done the exercise, can you see that "I" is a label and not an experiencer nor a thinker, not a doer nor hearer of rain? "I" is not what makes the eyes blink, and it is not a breather; it's a word used for the convenience of communication that refers to the speaker when she speaks about herself. If the "I" is believed to be an entity, the mind is confused, and the body tenses up. It is so simple. Bring attention back to now and look once again. Is there a *me* behind the word "me"? If so, where is it?

Life is happening. Looking is happening. Getting lost in the story is happening—with or without the word "I." The self is not needed for frustration to arise, nor for happy, joyful feelings. It all flows freely, as a response to a situation. Do we really need to be enslaved by labels? After all, experience is what labels point *to*. Labels do not own experience. The word "experience" is a label too.

And so the story goes on. Belief in the truthfulness of a story drops away. The story is way more enjoyable without the fear that something can happen to this "me." Once it's clearly seen that there is no actual me, there is no place for the story to stick. Whatever happens feels okay. Even being miserable. Confidence, grace, fearlessness, and peace with *what is* start to shine through as fear is loosened.

In a way it is funny! Imagine that! Humans got screwed by labels. Look at the world of fashion; labels are so important! So much emotional pain, such strong desire to get home, when home is all there is. Right here—underneath all the labels. Home is here, now, waiting to be recognized.

The Story and the Narrator

Being a human is somewhat like visiting an amusement park of life stories. Humans love stories; they find them to be a great source of entertainment. Look at the industries of movies, books, news, and gossip. Everyone loves a good, juicy story. And the best story is this exclusive story of [insert your name here]'s life being told. How fascinating.

We spend every minute thinking. Thoughts come as flashing images and sound like a never-ending commentary, describing, judging, evaluating, and analyzing what is going on. There is so much going on! In the story, the past, the present, and the future are all happening right now. There are so many associations, and so many emotions get stirred up. It's madness. And there are different voices, too—good and bad, wise and stupid. And they talk to each other and pretend to be different characters, replaying events and creating scenarios. A whole zoo.

Try This for Yourself   For just a minute, tell the voice in the head to be quiet, and see what happens.

The Stories in Our Head

The biggest part of everyday thinking is made up of stories about what is *not* happening here and now. The focus seems to stay on what is happening in the head, as this narrative appears to be the most important part of experience; it's composed of imaginary what-if scenarios, replays of arguments, daydreaming, remembering, planning, and looking for problems and possible solutions.

It's okay when the story is good. For some, for a short, quiet time the story is peaceful and exciting, blissful and great. But for many people, the stories are mainly about what is lacking: *I wanted this, but I'm not getting it,* with a hidden story underneath of *not being good enough,* or *not enough.* There are persistent stories about what is wrong with them, how it makes them feel, what needs to be fixed or avoided. The I Virus runs many different programs that filter information and determine what fits and what does not fit the current image of how things should be. Thinking is a constant game of find and fix a problem, and if you cannot find one, create one. It's a constant battle with reality. Struggle is at the forefront much more often than peace. Stories are patterns of thinking.

"I am not good enough" is a typical story; it's one of the main stories of human suffering.

I am not good enough.

It's a sad story about guilt—guilt for being yourself. As if being yourself is not enough! Can you see that the *sense of being* is here with or without the story?

It really is a joke—that story is only a pattern of thinking, a habitual thought, a verbal program that runs in the head. Do you ever stop and take a look to see if a thought is true? No, of course not, because thinking is so ingrained and familiar that it *seems* to be true. It's "truth" is confirmed by experience, and it does not even cross the mind to ever question whether what you think is true or not!

What Happens When You Simply Look?

Once you start looking at thinking really closely, a realization pops up into view: *the story is made up of thoughts about thoughts about thoughts.* It's thoughts all the way through.

What is it that is telling the story? Are you in control of what is being told? If not, then what is this voice in the head? What is it talking to and what is it that is listening? All that we hear is what it is talking *about*! Are you the one that talks or listens? Are you the owner of the voice? Are you the thinker of thoughts? Is the "I" the thinker or is it a thought? Where is the narrator? *Narrator, hello-o-o! Who's there? Anyone?*

> **Try This for Yourself**   Just for fun, or for curiosity's sake, ask that voice what it is and see what it says.
>
> Zoom in the focus on the commentator, and wait for the comments.
>
> If the voice suddenly shuts up, notice the silence.
>
> This silence is not the absence of an answer. Its message is simple: *there is no one here.* There is nothing fixed or solid there. Thoughts arise and pass away and happen to no one.
>
> What a shocker! It's funny and may even be a bit disappointing—and here you have another story already started in your head, but now it's a story about the silence…and the story is never ending. *Story* is like a ride in an amusement park without a get-off-the-ride button.

You see, there is no one behind the word "I." This word points at nothing other than a direction of what the story is about while communicating. (The story is about *me* and not Suzy, or Batman.)

The story is telling itself, and that's how it has always been. And when you take a look at that story with full attention and curiosity, it reveals what it is made of and how it's happening. This revealing is inevitable. It's the important part of the story, too.

Consider this: every story has a beginning, middle, and end. And the story is playing out, like programs, like spring-summer-autumn; there are patterns and seasons. Whatever story is playing out, the structure is the same. There's no skipping of parts. Time is an essential part of the structure or, should I say, an inevitable side effect.

If I look for a character, I see that there is this story about the life of Ilona: from birth to now, the biography of the character that tells which school I went to and what my classmates' names were and the year I graduated from university; then, that I moved to England and met these people, and that yesterday I saw a clown. There is this kind of neutral, innocent narration of events. *This* and *that* happened, with no emotions attached; the story is just the telling of events.

The story would be great if not for the sad narrator, who reminds you that you are not good enough, who reminds you of past mistakes. The judgmental comments create tension in the body and build craziness in the head. When the story becomes invested with emotion, thoughts trigger feelings, feelings get labeled and described. This creates more story, more feeling. This process is a self-supporting feedback loop. In other words, you get lost in the story.

Sometimes the story told by the narrator is about being great, being the most amazing and special person, one who has achieved so much, is victorious and so much better than others. These stories feed the ego, making one appear at the top, better and smarter than those undeserving others. It's a story of ownership, of specialness, of grandiose self-image that appears somehow precious and needs to be protected and sustained.

The commentary is just like a radio, but there is no choice of channels. You wish you could surf channels, because then your life would be great: all positive, fun, peaceful, and lovely. But you have only one channel, and it's telling the same old stories over and over again.

Imagine if you had only one TV channel, and you never switched the TV off. After a while there would be nothing interesting on; it would be the same old, same old, and the ads would drive you crazy. You'd try to ignore them and deny what is going on, or you'd talk back to the TV, but it would never occur to you that you could switch the TV off. You can, and you can also switch off the judge in the local radio station called "My Head."

The thing is, there is much more going on than just this one radio station. There is life happening—with and without the story, with and without the mental judge in the head. But since you are so absorbed in "my story," you miss what is right in front of your nose: There is no owner of the story. It simply is telling itself. There is no narrator at home.

And here comes that special thought: *Me. But what about me? I am here!*

This thought is like a bug in a computer program, the I Virus appearing as an entity, "me," who *seems* to be real.

So this *me* is believed to be most precious, a most carefully guarded thought, from which all thinking and doing happens. But thoughts cannot think; they cannot do anything other than appear and disappear. A thought is a tiny unit of information. *Me* is a thought, a thought pointing to other thoughts and images *about* a *me*. Where is *me* now? Don't just say, "There must be someone here!" Take a look and see what is true in experience, right here, right now.

Picture this: "Me" as a label on a box that contains all that is connected to the story of *me*, which is made up of feelings, memories, dreams, desires, fears, goals, and so on. Picture the big golden letters "ME." Looks good but…it's a mere tag. It's not an owner of content, not the manager of what happens in that content, not an entity; it's simply a concept, a name, an agreement to label these processes in one word: "me."

Can you see that humans spend their entire lives trying to improve and protect that "me"?

Try This for Yourself   Can comments be stopped at will?

Do you notice judgmental thoughts running?

Try to shut the judge up. Gag it if needed. Tell it to shut up. How long does that last? Test it for the fun of exploration.

Write down what feels true to you.

The sure way to see what is happening is to look closer at the mechanism of story in a spirit of curiosity.

How does story become so sticky?

Does it stick to the narrator?

What is the glue made of?

What drives it?

How do you step out of it?

I would say that the story becomes sticky when it is invested with emotion. The glue is made of belief. And the story is driven by emotion. Where the focus goes, story follows. But when focus goes onto the sensations, when the focus goes away from the head and into feeling and raw experiencing, release happens. Less story is being woven.

Stepping in and out of story is part of the dance of life. All is included.

Try This for Yourself   Here is another great question to ask when the story becomes too much: Is it true?

Is it true that a "me" exists? Is it true that there is no "I"?

Test it. Is it true that the story goes on by itself?

Employ this question often—use it!

There is a common assumption that seeing through illusion means that one does not get lost in the story ever again. If you continue to get lost in the story, then it may be time to take a careful look at why and how that's happening. But we do not need to get rid of the story. We merely need to see it as a fiction, not as true or imagined. The story is happening, yes; the content of the story is a story, not reality. All is not as it seems.

Ask yourself: Is it true that life goes on with or without the story? Are sounds and colors here if they don't have labels?

The story is part of life; it's a reflection of beliefs about life. Unquestioned assumptions play a crucial role in where and how the story goes.

Or so it seems.

Lakshmi

The following conversation with Lakshmi took place over several months. She wrote to me after reading my blog and was already investigating by herself. She was longing for joy of life and searching for happiness, just like many others. She was curious and did not sound desperate; the process of corresponding with her was light and seemed easy. When she realized the simplicity, and saw that no one owns feelings, she relaxed, and the search was over. Just like that. It was a pleasure to meet her and be able to assist.

Lakshmi: Hello, dear Ilona, I am Lakshmi from Hyderabad, India. I have been going through the articles in your blog for quite some time. I am also looking but maybe not deep, not sure!

Can you please guide and help me for the shift? Regards, Lakshmi.

Ilona: Hi Lakshmi. Thank you for your e-mail. Yes, we can have a conversation. Tell me a bit about your journey and where you are at the moment.

What are you looking for?

What do you expect from this process?

What do you think this will give you?

Take your time writing down all your expectations, and find those hidden ones too. Honesty is the key here. Looking forward to hearing from you. Kind regards.

Lakshmi: Hi Ilona. As I said earlier, ever since I was introduced to this technique, I have been trying to look at things around and yes, I could never find a separate "I" existing. It's always a thought. I am at this stage. I am able to appreciate the labeling that the mind does all the time. I am looking for "I" still, and expecting that I should feel light and easy sometimes. Maybe I am not looking enough, so not feeling it right away.

My expectations from this process are that I should be able to enjoy life, should be able to say that life is beautiful, as many realized people say it is after they got awakened to this truth of life. To be in the happy state irrespective of ongoing life. I have a habit of reacting to everything around, so I silently keep expecting this quality of mine to change after this process. I hope I spoke with honesty. Thanks and many regards.

Ilona: Hi Lakshmi. Thank you for your honest answer.

I am looking for "I" still, expecting that I should feel light and easy sometimes. Maybe I am not looking enough, so not feeling it right away.

What is it that you find when looking for "I"?

What is the first I in your sentence looking for "I"? What is it that you find when looking for "I"?

My expectations from this process are that I should be able to enjoy life, should be able to say that life is beautiful, as many realized people say it is after they got awakened to this truth of life.

That's all right.

To be in the happy state irrespective of ongoing life.

This is not realistic. There is no happily ever after. Life goes on as it does and things happen. It's not about a happy state at all. It's about seeing what is here now, already obvious. If you expect that seeing no self is going to give you eternal bliss, it's just a fantasy.

I have a habit of reacting to everything around, so I silently keep expecting this quality of mine to change after this process.

Reactions happen when buttons are pressed. While there are wounds, unresolved issues, and repressed feelings, of course, reactions will happen.

Before we go further, I'll ask you to leave all expectations behind. It is not what you expect at all. The mind can never imagine this. Having expectations is like trying to fit what is being seen into the frame of what it should look like. It's like looking at a picture of a square and imagining that you see a circle because it fits a current level of understanding.

Okay, tell me what comes up when you let this thought in: *There is no "I" at all, no separate self, no entity that is in charge of this piece of life, no manager, no controller, no doer, no thinker, no watcher. All there is, is life flowing freely as one movement.*

Write the reaction that comes up to this statement. Sending love.

Lakshmi: Hi Ilona.

What is it that you find when looking for "I"?

I find body, mind, senses existing and doing their job but can't find an "I" existing. I can see things existing everywhere around but can't see any "I."

What is the first I in your sentence looking for "I"? What is it that you find when looking for "I"?

Well, I really don't know, but it looks like this body-mind complex is the "I" which is looking for an "I." The mind which is working as "I"?!

Write the reaction that comes up to this statement.

I feel shocked, surprised; I feel it's such a joke that there is no self existing. I feel like laughing aloud. Feel sad, depressed too, feel painful, feel sick, feel *then, what now?* Oh my god. How could this be? This is what I feel as of now. Love, Lakshmi.

Ilona: Yeah, it's very simple and not even hidden.

Write more: What do you notice?

Was there ever an "I" there?

Sending love.

Lakshmi: I see, but yes, the "I" that is usually felt is the mind with this body, probably.

It is very strange to see the affairs happening around. Every concept and movement around revolves around this so-called "I." So much of identification which only gives temporary states of happiness, grief, and all other emotions.

What *are* all these faiths, beliefs, relationships for when there is no "I" existing?

Can the illusion of "I" be so powerful that it can dictate everything around?

It's relatively easy to *look* when I am in a happy or a neutral state, but *looking* is so difficult in an angry, sad, diseased, or suffering state. Only body, mind, senses, and memory exist and are felt and functioning all the time in the day-to-day affairs. From the childhood till the present moment, all that is registered through the senses in the memory is used for living, working, growing, and so forth. Emotions, behavioral patterns, movements are all happening from the stored memory, from conditioning. No one seems to be having any control over the inputs and the outputs of living and life. Everything is just happening and you are a part of it. Like a dry leaf which fell from the tree into the flowing water.

Some time later...

Lakshmi: Hi Ilona. Whatever I look at, I feel that—other than the existing fact, the picture or the sound—there is a constant labeling of the mind that goes on and on. The silence is broken with the constant chattering of the mind. The thoughts keep on coming from somewhere. When the senses are doing their job, the thoughts come from our saved memory, past, conditioning, expectations, and so forth. There was never an "I" because the "I" that was there when I was child was the label to this body-mind complex which is totally changed and different from what exists now. This can't be "I." Was there never any "I"? Thoughts, feelings, emotions, actions, reactions are happening as a game, as a sequence, as a jigsaw puzzle. It is just happening, going on and on. No one seems to be having any control. When there is no "I," then there is *only life* going on.

Ilona: Hi Lakshmi.

The silence is broken with the constant chattering of the mind.

Yes, there is a voice talking, labeling everything and telling stories.

The thoughts keep on coming from somewhere.

Take a good look—where are thoughts coming from? What is behind them? Is there a thinker?

When the senses are doing their job, the thoughts come from our saved memory, past, conditioning, expectations, and so forth.

So it appears, but have a closer look.

Is there "stored memory" in your experience?

Is there past? Future?

Is there a container that contains thoughts?

Is there anyone who the voice is talking to?

Is anyone listening?

Are you the voice that keeps talking?

Examine this closely and write to me the answers that feel true to each question. Sending love.

Lakshmi: Hi Ilona. Been busy last few days, but *looking* most of the time, and it's been a very lovely experience of feeling light. No emotions seem to be staying for long. The answers for the doubts that come up seem to be effortlessly flowing in and making it easy. It feels too good, trust me! Will write to you in more detail in the next two days. Thanks. Regards, Lakshmi.

Ilona: Sounds lovely! Tell me more.

Lakshmi: True, the life seems to happen, going on and on. But this mind takes charge, labels and tells stories all the time. It does appear there is a *thinker*, but that is again the mind which is saying "I" believe. The body, with the mind and senses, is the thinker, actor, feeler, reactor, and it all looks as if it projects and reacts, imagines, creates. Yes! Because otherwise there is no one! The world, the people, the relationships, and their qualities look like jigsaw puzzle pieces fitting into each other and collectively appearing as the world around. There is no *thinker*, except for the interference and chattering of the mind all the time. Oh, god! But the identification is too much; it appears as the only real thing existing and spins a web of a world around that "I." Yes, when I look, it seems to be clear. In spite of all this, it still becomes difficult to *look* in sad moods or so-called hurt moods and mad moods. Yes, the answer does come almost immediately. All the time, the question comes: *who is there to hurt, and who is there to get hurt?* Wow! Is this true? Is it getting clearer? Anyways, thanks Ilona!! Regards.

Ilona: Hi Lakshmi.

The body, with the mind and senses, is the thinker, actor, feeler, reactor, and it all looks as if it projects and reacts, imagines, creates. Yes!

So it appears! But, is it true?

Because otherwise there is no one!

Yes, there is no one. It's not that something is absent, there is nothing there, emptiness.

Yes, when I look, it seems to be clear.

See, every time you look it's clear. So keep looking in every situation where it appears that there is a doer, chooser, manager, and so forth. Each identification is an invitation to look deeper.

In spite of all this, it still becomes difficult to look in sad moods or so-called hurt moods and mad moods.

The thing with feelings is that all they want is to be felt fully and openly. There is no need to analyze feelings. It's an energetic thing going on. When you name the emotion, it appears solid. When you don't name it, it's a movement of sensation. Feel it as it comes, when it comes, and it will pass quickly. You don't need to do anything else. Just feel. Just watch the energy dance.

All the time the question comes: who is there to hurt, and who is there to get hurt?

There *is* no *who*. So asking the *who* question is in itself creating an illusion.

Is there someone or something that feels?

Is there an "I" here, right now?

Is there a doer of this action (reading these words right now)?

Is it getting clearer?

Yes! Keep digging. Much love.

Lakshmi: Hi Ilona. There seems to be nothing existing other than this body-mind complex and the world just runs on the constant chattering of the mind. *Mind.* Yes, *the mind* is the one that runs the world. Nothing else is present. The nonstop stories, expectations, chattering, commentary of the mind that's happening. Everything that's happening is just with this mind that's talking. The mind orders and the body reacts. The mind is conditioned day after day and it talks. Every being is a complex of body, mind, and senses together. No, there is no doer to this action of mine right now, whether it's reading the mail or typing it. Everything is happening. There is a continuous happening. All else is the commentary of the mind and not real. Thanks Ilona. Love.

Some time later…

Lakshmi: The "I" is just a thought from the mind. This thought is the strongest that can ever happen. Then, the drama of the mind unfolds around this "I." It's just too much. The world is but the combination of our thoughts, words, and actions. Thoughts mostly look like they are coming from somewhere not known.

Ilona:

There seems to be nothing existing other than this body-mind complex.

Really? So body exists and nothing else does? Interesting.

And the world just runs on the constant chattering of the mind. Mind. Yes, the mind is the one that runs the world. Nothing else is present.

What is this mind you are talking about?

What does the word "mind" point to?

The nonstop stories, expectations, chattering, commentary of the mind that's happening.

Are stories all there is?

Take a look at what is underneath the stories.

Does experience need stories in order to be happening?

Test with the senses. When you taste something, does the experience of tasting require a story to make it happen?

Get out of the head and into sensations and see what else is there.

The "I" is just a thought from the mind. This thought is the strongest that can ever happen.

No, it is not. It's an empty thought. What is it that makes it strong?

The world is but the combination of our thoughts, words, and actions.

The thoughts about the world create an image. But there is something else here besides a mind-created image in imagination.

What is here, now? Take a look.

Thoughts mostly look like they are coming from somewhere not known.

Take a good look.

Where are thoughts coming from?

Look till you see.

Lakshmi: No, the experience doesn't need any stories. The experience of tasting doesn't need a story, definitely. The experience is going on and will go on without all this commentary. The mind I meant is a bundle of thoughts. The body I meant is this physical body which I can see with the senses. The sensations are happening and *it* is happening. No stories or anything required for this. The "I" is just an empty thought but gets stronger with the stories, desires, expectations, and so forth. Yes, otherwise it is an empty thought. Will keep writing. Thanks, Lakshmi.

Ilona:

The mind I meant is the bundle of thoughts.

What is a bundle of thoughts? Is that not just another thought?

Check if there is some kind of container that holds thoughts in a bundle.

Have a good look; what is the "I" that sees?

What is seeing?

What is looking?

Is there a line between "I" and the senses in experience?

What is it that makes the I-thought stronger?

These are a few more questions to play with. Sending love.

Lakshmi: Hi Ilona. Yes, there is no container of thoughts, definitely. It's just another thought or a label given to the thoughts that flow, probably. No, neither the "I" nor the senses seem to be existing as such except that the actions are happening and the labeling goes on, which we express in words and names. No, there is no line. The senses are acting, the actions are happening, and the rest is the labeling or the commentary. Will write more. Thanks, love.

Ilona: Dear Lakshmi, Good work. Let's explore language today. Notice how language creates a doer that is doing the action. See how the subject is part of labeling action.

I breathe—breathing is happening. Is it "I" that does breathing?

Does it matter which words describe experience?

Does description affect what is happening?

There is a labeling exercise on my blog [see page 76 in this book]. Please do it and write to me with what you noticed. Explore language through the day while talking to people, listening, reading, and so on. Sending love.

Lakshmi: Hi Ilona. Yes, I just did the exercise in the post that you sent. When I was doing the first part, I felt a sort of palpitation and pain here and there. When I did the second part, there was a sort of emptiness and hollowness and vacuum in the body, as if it was all empty inside. What I felt at the end, when I compared, is that actions happen without me and are happening anyway and are truer than the actions *with* me because labels are not affecting the experience and are only used for describing. "I" is just used for communication, description. It doesn't have any existence. Love, Lakshmi.

Ilona: Nice! Yes, description is practical and useful in communication. :) You are getting close.

How about the word "I"?

Is it empty or does it point to a separate entity that life is happening to?

When the word "I" is used in the description of what is happening, does it mean that the entity appears?

Sending love.

Lakshmi: Hi Ilona. The word "I" is definitely empty, except that it is used for communication or refers to that particular body-mind complex. It is empty because things happen whether or not it is used. "I" is another thought, and with a big commentary around it constantly. "I" refers to no entity. Nothing appears or disappears with "I." Whatever is there, is there irrespective of "I." Whatever has to happen will be happening. Love, Lakshmi.

Ilona: Yes!

How does it feel to see this?

Are you noticing anything different in everyday experience?

Can you say that, yes, it is clear, there is no separate entity "I." If not, is there anything else that needs to be looked at?

Sending love.

Lakshmi: Yes, Ilona, things are different in everyday experience. The answers especially seem to be flowing the moment a question arises in day-to-day incidents. The same thing is proven again and again, that it is all a game of the mind. As of now, I don't feel like there is a separate "I," but sometimes at times of hurt the "I" seems real until looking happens again. Thanks so much. How could you make this all so simple? I know there is no one to make it happen, *It happens.* Please help till the Gate is crossed. Much love.

Ilona: Hi Lakshmi. Keep looking.

What is behind the hurt when it arises?

See how it passes when it's noticed. The mind is checking this in every situation. "I" is never real. Sometimes it's a habitual assumption that comes back, but as you notice when looking, it's never found. After a while this looking drops. But don't wait for it. It may take a long time, or not. The hurt is a reaction to a touch of a painful spot. You may look at it and thank it for showing up. It's an opportunity to release it rather than resisting. Instead of the usual no, you can start saying yes to intense feelings, and just feel them openly. Each reaction is an invitation to look. Feelings pass quickly if there is no grasping.

Surrendering is what is left when resistance to *what is* ends.

When feelings arise, give them space. Feel them, honor them.

Are there separate entities in other people?

How do you see your closest ones?

How about strangers on the street?

Much love.

Lakshmi: Amazing! Superbly told! Will answer these questions soon. Thanks, regards. Love.

Later...

Yes, the hurt just passes when I start looking through. It is taking time to look during those times.

Things changed, Ilona, and it's just superb—is it so simple? There is—no "I." *Yes!* The reactions are passing easily, feeling light. No, there cannot be any separate entities in other people, just the same body-mind complex...differently conditioned, so reacting differently. Otherwise the machines are the same. Yes, my closest ones and the strangers are the same as I described, but with the close ones there is this body attachment with love and other feelings. It feels easy to understand everyone, closest ones and strangers, because it's all happening and there is no one to do anything. Thanks. Love.

Ilona: Sweet! Yes, there is no one here doing anything. All is one movement of life.

Are you ready for the final questions?

If not, what else we can look at?

Sending love.

Lakshmi: Hi Ilona, Want to look into few more aspects before the final ones! Will keep writing. Thanks for all this. Love.

Ilona: Share with me what you are noticing. Love.

Lakshmi: Hi Ilona. Been looking! Just a few thoughts that I would like to share. The questions about the horrible things that happen around us in this world disturb me. Like the rapes, murders; these things hurt and make it difficult to understand that things happen and deeds are done but there is no doer! Well, as I write, thoughts come that say, *yes, this is it*, but the doubting mind interferes. But, Ilona, I can't stop saying that this is an amazing drama unfolding in front of our eyes—and you made it so simple. Please tell me what it is that I need to do for that final step.

What is all this? Feeling responsible, sacrificing, and so on which are used so much in the Indian context—are they man-made? Good and bad? Help and hurt? They vary according to people, situations, and all sorts of factors. These things are confusing when looked at. Yes, all this is the mind chattering, and the actions are a result of the conditioning. All actions are the result of those thoughts over which there is no control, and then there are the reactions to all these actions. It looks like a cycle.

Later…

I am ready for the final questions.

Ilona: I'm very happy to hear that you are ready for the last questions. If something is not clear, answers will let me see that. Here are the questions…

Please answer in full, when ready.

Much love.

Lakshmi: Hi Ilona. Firstly, thank you, for all this.

1. Is there a separate entity "self," "me," "I" at all, anywhere, in any way, shape, or form? Was there ever?

No, there is no self, I, or me anywhere. Life is going on according to how it is supposed to be. There are different body-mind organisms, each with its own conditioning, programming, and memory just doing what has to be done all around. Other than this, there is no separate I, me, or self. Yes, there was an "I" before I started looking for it. The "I" that was there was what I thought was the life force which made my body move and the mind think. That consciousness is still there, but there is no "I" now. That consciousness is not separate, it is universal and is *there*. That's it.

2. Explain in detail what the illusion of separate self is, when it starts, and how it works from your own experience. Describe it fully as you see it now.

The illusion of separate self is that *I am a separate entity and I exist and I am the doer.* Maybe it starts from the time our mind starts thinking, working even as a child. It makes me feel that I am a separate individual and I am responsible for my actions, to plan, to think, to expect, to see good and bad. Label.

Now, I see it as just a *thought*, a mind projection—that's all. It only exists as a thought. I can't find it otherwise, neither in me nor others. Everyone seems to be a programmed machine consisting of body and mind working, according to the circumstances.

3. How does it feel to see this? What is the difference from before you started this dialogue? Please report from the past few days.

It feels very light, beautiful, because there is no burden of any doership in me, no "I" even in others. So there is no one doing anything to anyone. The answers come so easily to the questions which arise in day-to-day life. The perception changed and can't believe that it is so simple.

There are no serious complaints, no burdens, no serious goals, no feeling hurt like before. Mostly now (but not always) there's no holding anyone responsible for their deeds. Because every answer flows in and balances the emotion. I am sorry, I hope you can understand what I mean.

4. What was the last bit that pushed you over? What made you look?

Can't really pinpoint the last bit because every step kept pushing. Looking and looking at every step possible helped me. Looking especially when I am hurt helped me to realize and understand better. I am sorry that I am unable to pinpoint the last bit.

5. Do you decide, intend, choose, control events in life? Do you make anything happen? Give examples from your experience.

Oh, no! I definitely cannot control. Of course, I cannot even decide, intend, choose, because they all happen according to the circumstances and conditioning, which are just not in my control.

Like some of the experiences in life, when I look at the past: I always wanted to become a doctor and practice. Yes, I did become a doctor, but I am not practicing as I thought I would. I'm sitting at home and taking care of the kids and other family members because I lost my dad and brother at a crucial stage in my life. Life is just flowing with *no me*, no deciding, no choosing, no control, though the mind seems to be doing this by saying, *I exist*—but I now realize that this is also just another thought. Many incidents of life in the past and the present show that life just happens. The one quote that just keeps ringing in my ears is: *Events happen, deeds are done, but there is no doer.* And no doer means no "I," no separate self. This incident of meeting you, writing to you, looking at life, all this also is *happening*. Thanks and much love.

Ilona: Beautiful, thank you for answers, Lakshmi. I would like you to take a look a little bit closer:

Was there ever an "I"?

What is the "I" that was looking for "I"?

I can see that a shift has happened, just need to look a bit more.

Everyone seems to be a programmed machine consisting of body and mind working, according to the circumstances.

Yes, you can say that, but…

Zoom out a bit, look at the totality of movement, including this body. Is there a line between this machine and another machine?

Is it body that is experiencing and reacting?

Is there a line between reaction and circumstances?

When you look at what is looking, what is there?

Much love!

Lakshmi: Hi Ilona. "I" is another thought looking for "I"; it's all the mind that's working, thought by thought. All thoughts are coming as questions and answers too. There was never an "I." There is a separation in terms of bodies, but otherwise the rest is all the same—the functioning is the same. The thoughts which come are beyond control of any machine, and when there is no "I" for me then there is not any other "I." The experiences and reactions are happening according to the thoughts that come from somewhere over which there is no control; it's the thought of "I" that is reacting because of the identification with body. Yes, the circumstances are already there, beyond control. The reaction comes because of the "ego," the thought "I," the identification. There is no one who is looking, looking is happening. Thank you so much. Love, Lakshmi

Ilona: Thank you for answers. Hmm… There is something subtle that I invite you to look at. You say, *It's the thought of "I" that is reacting because of the identification with body.*

Say the word "I" loudly or quietly a few times. Is this thought reacting?

Can a thought identify with body?

What is it that identifies with the body?

What is behind identification?

Can you look closer here, is there an ego?

Or just more thoughts?

What do you notice?

Sending love.

Lakshmi: Hi Ilona, No, the thought isn't reacting. There is no identification. There is no one at all. Only more and more thoughts, that's all. There is *no one*. Oh my god!! Yes, *no one* indeed. Love, Lakshmi.

Ilona: That is it, and all is functioning just fine… Welcome home. And you know, it's just a beginning, a fresh start to new way of living.

I'm delighted for you.

I usually put these conversations on the blog. Would it be okay with you? I can use your name or any other name you prefer. If other guides have questions, they may ask. If not, I will invite you to join Liberation Unleashed Facebook groups.

Sending love!

Lakshmi: Thank you, Ilona, The journey has been beautiful. You can do whatever you feel like with the conversations and my name. Much love.

Ilona: Hi Lakshmi. Thank you so much. Have a wonderful day! Much love.

Some time later…

Lakshmi: Hi Ilona. It feels good to write, actually. To be frank, it is unbelievable that it is over, the seeking. Oh my god! How could it happen, and through you! Thanks for it. Anyways, it's been too good. I should say, especially, the load we carry in our hearts is almost nonexistent and just too light because there is no past, no future. There is no guilt, hatred, sin, or pride because you know that there is no one to feel all these. In my personal life, too, it's been a wonderful feeling of lightness. Freedom in all relationships, including parenting. Yes, the reactions do happen in every incident, but nothing really sticks. Many times I have heard in spiritual context that one needs to be like a flute: hollow for god to sing through. *Now* I understand its significance and meaning. What it means to be and live like that. Seeking has ended, and that is really comforting. Deep Looking helped to see and feel this, and now anything I see, anywhere I see, it just gets proven again and again that there is no one. It's so simple, but awesome!

To add some more feelings. All this process and post-process is beautiful... There is no more seeking, no more questions. The answers are flowing as if a blockage is being removed from a pipe. My god, this is too good! The feeling of a big puzzle being solved. The totality of life might be too big to understand, but the questions exist no more. *There is no one!* Life is much lighter and easygoing. The so-called negative qualities like anger, jealousy, and greed do not stay at all. Reactions continue but they are less severe and very transient. Nothing affects. Feels like laughing out loud a lot of times.

Thanks again, Ilona, because all this happened through your guidance.

Love, Lakshmi.

Thinking

I talk to a lot of people about thinking, and I feel like sharing some ideas with you. Of course, all of this is subjective. It's for you to see for yourself.

People hear that if they can only stop thinking, all will be experienced more deeply and vividly, and they will be more aware. I receive questions all the time from people asking me how they can stop the labeling, the never-ending stream of thoughts. People try many things: meditation, willpower, and generally hating the voice in the head because it talks so much.

Thoughts are not a problem. Thinking that thoughts are the problem *is* the problem. See? People get locked in a repeat loop when they don't realize the true nature of the problem.

Thinking is innocent, and it's a great tool in a practical sense and in terms of artistic expression and entertainment. It is part of experience, part of the whole—there's no need to try to get rid of it. And you can't get rid of it if you try. Just sit for half an hour trying not to think, and see how that goes.

Belief Is Composed of Thoughts About Thoughts

Believing in the truthfulness of thoughts, and taking them seriously, gets in the way of peace—most of the time. Belief is made up of thoughts agreeing with repetitive thoughts; it's a self-reinforcing feedback loop that stays in the system until properly examined. Beliefs are the core around which experience organizes itself. What happens when they are examined properly? See for yourself. Watch the thinking process, and notice how it happens.

Thoughts are symbols, labels; they form descriptions and interpretations of experience. Thoughts that are believed create tension and resistance as well as clinging and attachments. The I-thought seems to claim doership of thinking and action. But "I" is just a thought, like any other thought; it is not the I-thought that is thinking. Thinking is not done by you, it happens just like rain: rain is not rained by a cloud, it rains. There is no "rainer."

Thank Thoughts, Don't Fight Them

Rather than fighting thoughts, rather than hating this labeling process that goes on automatically, *thank them!*

Seriously, thank the mind for coming. Literally say, "Mind, I love you. You have been such a great mind, working so much for me. I really appreciate you. You are a gorgeous, beautiful, curious, caring, innocent mind! I love you!"

Instead of working against what is happening, turn your reaction around and see what happens. I'm not going to *tell* you—have a look for yourself to see how this response works. One thing is for sure: the mind will respond. And you can talk to it as you would a child. You don't have to believe me: test it—see if it works for you.

Shoulds, Should Nots, and Wants

Thoughts that say what should and should not happen are weeds in your thought garden. When you notice them, stop and make a mental note; see if the opposite of "should" and "should not" is true, too. These thoughts create more thoughts about what is wrong. Notice them.

When shoulds and should nots are cleared, look out for "wants." You will notice these mostly in certain areas, such as security, control, love, and acceptance. The wants are weeds, too, but somehow they are more difficult to let go of. Spend a day, or a few, taking your time to catch that word "want" every time you say or think it. Just make a mental note of when it shows up and in what situation. There is no need to follow these thoughts, just recognize when they are happening. Thank the wants for coming, too. It is okay to want what you want. You don't have to do anything about it.

I call *shoulds* and *wants* "mind weeds" because these kinds of thoughts have great expansion potential. If you give them attention, they grow into more elaborate thoughts very quickly and are emotionally charged. They are clingy and sticky. Shoulds are thoughts of expectation, and wants are thoughts of lacking, of seeking something.

It's not that these thoughts should not be coming up. When they come up, welcome them, because they will come up until you drop them or inspect them. Instead, welcome them, because they can show limitations and restrictions that are still in the system. Releasing shoulds and wants opens the mind to seeing *what is* and allows it to be at ease.

So, to sum up, instead of trying to get rid of thoughts, welcome them. Instead of holding on to shoulds, let them go; notice wants, and honor the mind.

The Description Is Not the Experience

Clarity comes when the description of what was experienced is not understood to be *all* experience. Thinking in and of itself is not the totality of experience; there is also perception through the senses and through feeling. If all focus goes to thinking, then the rest of experience is missed. And then you live in your head, lost in thinking, analyzing, and endlessly trying something mental. This is hard, and it's unnecessary too.

Imagine you get a gift wrapped in nice paper, and all of your attention is focused on the wrapping. You are so attached to the paper, the ribbon, and the bow that you don't even notice the gift. Then you get another gift and another, and still the wrapping job is all you ever see. Thoughts are to experience as that wrapping is to the gift.

When the mind is clear, it does not confuse the description of experience with real experience, words for things, or the map for the territory. The fog, the veil that seems to be in the way of seeing, is made up of descriptions, of labels given to the whole experience. The silent experiencing through feelings and sensations is left in the background, unnoticed, ignored. Life cannot be experienced fully and richly if one is living a story about the present moment rather than living the present moment that is so full and rich in sensations. *Trying* to stay in the present moment takes a huge amount of energy. *Noticing* presence here and now is effortless.

Try This for Yourself   Take something from your immediate environment and smell it. Whatever is right here, right now, inhale the scent.

Hold it, feel it, and experience it. Smell that thing for two minutes. Take your time with experiencing; don't pay attention to labels, rather experience the sensation.

For the next two minutes, describe the experience verbally and fully.

This test illustrates the difference between experience and description. But wait! Describing experience is also an experience, a fresh one happening in the moment.

Experiencing thinking is as real as experiencing smelling and other senses. If you pay attention and look deeply, thinking is happening; it is about experiences, and that in and of itself is experience. As you can see, the wrapping is also part of the gift.

Vision, hearing, tasting, touching, and smelling are the five channels through which data enters your experience. Thinking is what makes sense of the data; it interprets the data and describes what is going on, putting it all into a *story*. This process can be useful and practical, or it can just be unnecessary and useless.

The Mind and the Heart

Some thoughts trigger feelings. This is another channel of perception—the channel of the heart. When the mind and heart work in balance, there is joy and peace, there is openness and expansion. When the heart is closed or hurt, the mind is "in charge," working hard to protect that which "needs" to be protected, with the help of a loyal friend called "fear." The mind has a lot to do, a lot to keep track of, and it gets very busy, exhausting itself till it shuts down or explodes in a mental display of frustration.

The mind thinks that it has to understand and control everything, because it thinks that is its job. It thinks. But is it true that the mind is really in charge of life?

When the mind is relaxed, it's great; it's like a joyful kitten, curious, innocent, playful, and fun, or silent and peaceful. The mind is afraid of losing its job micromanaging the universe. As if it is really doing that. It pretends that it is the manager of what happens and forgets that all of this is just a play.

The misunderstanding that the thinking mind is the primary and most important channel of perception is with us until we see that nothing controls *what is*. Everything simply happens. Life is going on by itself, including thinking about how this "me" is in charge. There is no thinker, no doer, so there is no one in control. Life flows freely, even if it does not seem this way.

Be kind to the mind. Let it know that you appreciate it. And let it slowly retire from the assumed position of the General Manager of the Universe. It will return to being the innocent mind that is creative, curious, and joyful. You won't need to try to shut it up. It loves silence.

Love the mind and be kind to it, soften up. Just for a day, appreciate it, and say yes to the voice in the head. Kindness is soothing and leads to an opening. See if doing these things makes a difference for you.

What Do You Really Want?

There may be many things that you want. Let's have a look at a few: control, security, and acceptance.

Look a little bit closer at these things that many people desire. And try the following exercise.

> **Try This for Yourself**   For a day or two, just watch the wanting that comes up.
>
> In what area does it show up the most?
>
> Where is the biggest lack felt?

You don't need to do anything but notice and acknowledge. Watch what happens, and notice how it feels. Feel the gap between wanting and not having, and observe what sensations are triggered when wanting appears. Bringing attention to the mechanism of wanting will reveal curious things.

Wanting Control

Control is one of the main human wants—wanting to be in charge, powerful, and right. Wanting to have control over actions, thoughts, and feelings is the driving force that moves actions in a particular way. Wanting control is the flip side of lacking control. Wanting is a sign that something is incomplete, or missing.

Here is another angle. Wanting control is just that—*wanting*. Spontaneous actions are happening, and so is the thought story. The narrator tells the story in first person: How I *did this* and I *did that*, owning the deeds, presenting himself or herself as the creator,

the master of body, the thinker of thoughts. *I* am the good guy or
the bad guy, depending on the situation.

There is a story about trying to be in control and not succeeding
and the feelings of guilt and shame that arise with the failure. It is
interesting to watch how all this works, how thoughts of lacking and
wanting create a ripple of sensations, and how you can't control any
of it. Sensations arise; take a look at them. Which one of them is
the sensation of "being in or out of control"? Can you pinpoint it?
What is that sensation without the label?

In simple everyday life, what is happening is happening.
Decisions are made, actions are taken, things get done. Thinking
about what should be done, thinking about what needs to be done,
and planning the next step flow with whatever is happening. Hands
and feet are doing their thing and thoughts are flying by.

What is in control of that? Think about it. If I ask "What is in
control of the weather?," what would your answer be? Thoughts?
Clouds? Or maybe the wind?

Wanting to be in control is painful. One is trying to get all the
ducks in a row all the time. The environment and others must be
controlled, otherwise…unwanted emotions will arise, and that
means suffering.

The end of trying to change *what is* starts with seeing that the
doer is imagined. Still, though, actions are taken and choices are
made with or without the narration of events. So what? The story
continues. When a story is seen as a story, not actuality, it can carry
on without making things and events overly serious and dramatic.
The story can be taken lightly; it can be entertaining and fun, as
well as serious when a situation asks for seriousness.

I find that if I don't take action when "wanting control" shows
up, the focus shifts to something else. This pattern needs to be seen,
then it can drop away. Then one can relax into being and enjoy
what is happening, rather than trying endlessly to make things go in
a particular way and becoming upset when they don't.

The ride does not care how the passenger feels about what is happening; it carries on regardless. The passenger, however, cares about the ride—especially if she thinks she's the driver.

Wanting Security

Wanting security comes with thoughts about time. Wanting security has to do with thoughts or fear about the future. The mind creates endless what-if scenarios about how the future is uncertain, unwelcome, and scary. The fear of the unknown is at the root of wanting security. Interestingly, fear shows up when thoughts about the future come up. If there is no anxiety about what will be, then security is not an issue.

Fear and security are different ends of the same stick. They are connected to projections of an imagined outcome. If you stopped thinking about what may happen and paid attention to what is actually happening right here, right now, there wouldn't be any room for fear; there wouldn't be any need to protect a self-image from things that may or may not happen.

Consider this: the future never comes—all we have is now. Thinking about problems does not always solve problems, it mostly creates them. Thinking about the past or future creates a sensation that there is a lack of safety. It can drive you nuts. All of this is happening in the mind, not in reality, so stop it. Don't pour petrol onto the fire when fearful thoughts come up. Don't feed the stories with more stories. Instead, focus on the sensations that are happening now; let them be seen, and let them pass. Out of curiosity, look behind the fear. What is it trying to protect?

Wanting Love and Acceptance

Wanting to be loved, acknowledged, validated, heard, respected, honored, accepted, and cherished are big wants. It's common to think that love and acceptance have to come from someone else, from outside; only then, you imagine, will you be happy and feel loved. But the love you seek is really love for yourself. There is no one person out there who can give it to you. The heart wants to love freely, openly, and limitlessly. The heart opens when conditions are right. I will talk more about this in the "Deep Looking" chapter and give you guidelines on how to listen to the heart and hear what it really wants.

Other Wants

Other common wants include living in the present, being yourself, living fully, not wanting, stopping searching, and knowing. You can examine the field of attachments, wants, and desires yourself. If there is action you can take when a want comes up, then take it. If not, just watch, smile, take notes, and release.

Shanti

I communicated with Shanti over the course of two weeks. She e-mailed me when she was already in the looking process, so it was a focused and quick conversation. The last boundary she needed to see through was fear about her children. She was afraid that she would lose them if the truth was realized. It did not take her long to face that fear and drop it. It was very interesting to hear that, despite the fact that she was a facilitator for Scott Kiloby's The Living Inquiries, she was still looking for answers and getting angry about not "getting" it. Finally, after years of seeking, the home was found over the course of our correspondence. The simplicity finally came. I was very happy for Shanti that our inquiry worked.

Shanti: Hello. I am in Switzerland and am at the Gate, would love some midwifery. Do you do Skype sessions?

Ilona: Hi Shanti. Thanks for the message. I don't do Skype sessions at the moment; I prefer e-mail or the forum. Whichever works for you. Kind regards.

Shanti: I have a difficult time with words, plus I am lazy—let's give e-mail a try. I will begin tomorrow. Is this okay for you? Is there anything I need to know? Thank you.

The next day…

Shanti: Good morning. It simply begins. There is much that has been undone, or that unraveled. The concept of no choice, of the "I," yet there is anger mostly directed at my four children. It is intense and it hurts at times. It is so much different than before, but there is still this idea that they are "mine" and I am responsible for feeding them, taking care of them and raising them. There is still a sense of separateness. Confusion mostly, and some fear. Thank you.

Ilona: Hi Shanti. Of course a mother will take care of her children, and there is no doubt about strong connection and love. That is how life is, in nature too, the mother cares about her children. It does not mean, though, that she owns them. Does your mother own you? The anger is a response to triggers. If you hurt your leg and somebody kicks it by accident, naturally it will hurt and there will be a response, a reaction, perhaps anger. It hurts, because it's wounded. So there is also a reaction when emotional wounds are touched or pressed on. That is, until they heal and no longer trigger any reaction. This process is about seeing what is really going on in your experience. It does not fix anything, nor change how things are. Only lets you see for yourself, by yourself, how it all works. If you are looking to fix something or get rid of anger, this process is not about that. If you want the truth, no matter what, and are ready to question your most precious beliefs, then we can work together.

On the scale from 1–10, how ready are you?

What is it that you are looking for?

Sending love.

Shanti: Yes. It more feels like the mother thing is too much, a "so much responsibility and freedom is hard to find" kind of a reaction. I am ready. 10. I am done seeking, looking has begun. The "I" doesn't think, and I think that I am either at the Gate or over it. I see that there is no "I," there is, however, still a sense of "self" being a mother, for example, or a person who needs/wants to make money to pay bills. When I first approached you, I think I was looking for some kind of answer. It is not like this anymore. It feels more like a settling in, and I want to make sure that a sense of self lingers. Gratitude for you.

Ilona: Hi Shanti. Thank you for the e-mail, I see you are ripe and ready.

So you say that "I" does not think; can it cross the Gate?

What is the "I" that you are referring to?

What are the expectations at this point?

Does the sense of aliveness or being have to cease?

Are you waiting for some state or big experience?

It may or may not happen and it isn't a necessary part of the process. The shift may be so subtle that it may be hard to notice. What is it that sees that there is no "I"?

Write soon.

Shanti:

What is it that sees that there is no "I"?

Phew! I have no idea: eyes, looking? It has been subtle—prior to the shift there was a lot of anger and resistance and tantrum throwing. A lot! And then I noticed, *Hmm. "I" doesn't think, drink, eat, sleep. It is a thought just like all the others.* There was laughter, and, *Holy crap, is this it?* Cool. And then the children and contraction and the idea that something has to stay, like the laughter has to be permanent or something that could care less. The sense that "I" *has* to be here, even if I see that it isn't. In my immediate experience there is no one here and yet there's also a sense that I will find her if I just wait long enough. Have you ever gone looking for your keys or something you were sure you knew where you left them, and after a while of looking you experience frustration, irritation maybe. *Damn, I know they are here somewhere.* Then you find them in your pocket and you laugh out loud. Yep, that simple—yet, not totally. It seems like layers are peeling away effortlessly and it *should* be hard and deep and whiz bang boom.

Ilona: Sweet! *It* should *be hard.* Ha ha, but yes, so simple. It's like looking for home while being at home. No-step journey. Finding home is just noticing that you have never left home.

About the children, is it possible to stop caring about them?

Are they separate from you?

Is there an "I" in each of them?

Much love.

Shanti: No, not possible to stop caring about them. There is no "I" in any of them. Are they separate from me? Hmm, seems like it at the moment in my current experience. They don't even exist, so this *is* strange, there is a sense that they are somehow separate, but also not. Loving you.

Ilona: Separation is only a thought.

Take a look with the senses, each one individually.

Is there anything separate in hearing?

Is there a gap between the hearer and the sound?

Is there anything separate in the view when you look with eyes closed and when you look with eyes open?

How about touch? Feel the sensation of touch and see if there is a gap between experienced and experiencer.

Look at nature, spend some time watching the movement of totality. Is there anything incomplete or independent of everything else?

Write to me soon. Much love.

Shanti: Hearing happens. Viewing happens. No separation between hearer/hearing or viewing/viewer or feeler/felt. No gap between experiencer/experienced. In nature there appear to be separate "things"—birds *in* the sky, clouds *in* the sky, wind *in* the trees or *on* the skin. Trees *in* the ground and the sky or surrounding landscape; all of it being experienced *together.*

In my home there are my children, my husband, and they appear to be separate, but they are *not* separate. They exist because I do. The experience *of* them would not take place without *me* experiencing them. There are thoughts that this just doesn't make any sense, this appearance of separation, the apparent others, and some settling of this "knowing." There is less and less of the sense of actual separation, so many ideas of what I thought not experiencing separation would be like. So many fantasies falling away. Good. Big love.

Ilona:

Hearing happens. Viewing happens. No separation between hearer/ hearing or viewing/viewer or feeler/felt. No gap between experiencer/ experienced. In nature there appear to be separate "things"—birds in the sky, clouds in the sky, wind in the trees or on the skin. Trees in the ground and the sky or surrounding landscape; all of it being experienced together.

It is only language that makes the experienced appear separated. When you see the bird in the sky, there is a movement of shapes and colors, labels come up—"bird," "sky," "in."

Can you experience a bird without sky, outside of sky (while looking up)?

It's just like saying that the grass is growing and assuming that there is something called grass that does the growing. It's one indivisible whole, which can only be divided by words; words that are believed to be real things, objects.

In my home there are my children, my husband, and they appear to be separate, but they are not separate. They exist because I do. The experience of them would not take place without me experiencing them.

Yes. Good stuff. Here is an article for you called "The Trick of Language" [included in this book, in the chapter "Concepts, Words, and Stories Are Not What They Seem"] and an exercise in the follow-up post on my blog. Do it properly and write to me after—what you noticed, how the description of what is happening affects what's happening. Love back to you.

Shanti: I will write tomorrow, I think. Feeling a little sick. Earlier I felt I had a lot to respond with. It went away though. Thank you.

Ilona: Hope you are feeling better. Sometimes the process can be very intense and the body can be going through stress. Disillusionment can be accompanied by purging—intense burning in the body and flu-like symptoms. If it's happening, rest a lot and let the process take care of itself. It's all part of it. It will pass. Just let it all be okay. Sending love to you.

Shanti: Thank you, good to hear. Physically, the last eight months or so have been interesting to say the least. I am a mover, I train the body a lot because I like to, not to achieve anything. But it has been hard going these last eight months, catching almost all colds and viruses. Not just me, my whole family. Sleep is good, when I get it (I'm often up with sick kids), but I've had nightmarish dreams the last two months. Otherwise peaceful sleep, no spinning just sleeping. Your words are like a salve, letting me know that this experience is just happening. No one to blame, nowhere to look to make it better. Ironically, at the moment, the "sickness" feels like a relaxation with a bit of resistance, or better said "residue," showing up physically.

I would like to share a bit of my process with you. I am thirty-seven. Two years ago I went to The School for The Work with Byron Katie [see http://thework.com] and the veils really began to drop. Prior to that experience, I didn't know anything about non-duality, enlightenment, awakening—nada. I didn't even know that thoughts aren't real. I did The Work for one year, every day, almost all day. Then, like most things, it dropped away. Life felt easy, effortless, it was nice.

Then—well I don't know exactly what happened, but it felt like I fell out of that experience and there was a series of events that took me into the deep dark uglies, real bad. There was deep depression and sickness that was followed by rage and pissed-offness—it was intense, and it's only in the last two weeks that it seems to have subsided. During the darkness, I became a facilitator for the Scott Kiloby "Inquiries." I just got more and more pissed off and had a feeling I was getting so close to seeing "the holy grail," whatever the hell that was. I just got fuckin' pissed and fed up with *looking*. Looking at words, images, sensations and looking for some self and not being able to find it, ever. Thinking the looking was going to kill me. There is a huge difference between looking and seeing. This I have experienced.

Then a very dear friend of mine sent me your book on whatever day it was that I contacted you. I had been feeling like I needed support of some kind, someone to help me *see* what I was already seeing and experiencing. Honestly, someone who would validate what I was/am experiencing, like giving me a home until I really could see I am already home. That person right now is *you*. Deep gratitude. Language is something I see through quickly in the moment and I could easily fall into a space where communication would get really weird, but we seem to have overcome the paradox of using I, you, we, us, me, which is strange but useful. Verbing is all that is really going on.

Many things you have said, I have experienced but then not *seen*, if that makes any kind of sense. Yesterday, as I read your book, reading stopped and all desire to read such books left; there's a movement away—and just now, as this e-mail is being written, there is movement to prepare lunch. There is no one doing it. It is just happening. I have been pointing for others for a long time and I just didn't know that that was what I was doing. Now the happenings seem to make some kind of sense.

I most definitely thought there would be some big boom and now I notice so many misconceptions and misunderstandings—not the least of which is being Shanti. She is the confusion, the compromise that was created to fit in, out of love, yet meaningless. Applying this to my children has been so interesting; they too are a story. Without the story, they just *are*. I have no idea if this is making any sense; thank you for reading so far. There are silly questions still about time and money but they come and they go as if I cannot grab on to them at all. Falling away.

It seems to be smoothing out, whatever that means, strange and totally normal somehow. So much stuff falling away. Thank *you*, me…I…it…everything…life…happening!

Ilona: Thank you so much for sharing your story, it's quite something. I'm so happy to hear that you are relaxing. Yes, the shift is so small, subtle, ordinary, and yet all starts to look different. Where you thought that you needed to get home, there is noticing, that home is here, now, always.

How are you feeling? Yes, falling can be intense, just allow all to pass. Holding on is not advisable. Lots of love.

Shanti: How am I feeling? As if the fan is slowing down, the stirring, the spinning of the mind, how to explain? It is as if something is alive and living thoughts cannot be held on to, no matter what. Anger happens, irritation happens, overwhelm happens, and yet it doesn't. It is *wild*. Like the last remnants of firecrackers, pop…pop… fizzle. Perhaps this is the settling in, the sinking in, the falling away of stuff. It feels somehow stable, constant. Where it used to come and go, it now seems to be constant and not able to be unseen. Deep, flowing, intense desire and excitement to *share* with others. That is how Shanti expresses, she is a sharer. But this, well this is different. This experience is for everyone. No one is a guru or special. All the same. The experience belongs to no one and to everyone. Hope this makes sense. Would love to connect with others to point wherever possible. Thank you for *all* that you are.

There is something interesting and at the same time meaningless. This way of looking. I sucked it all in or out or whatever. Is so darn simple, it seems that inquiry and religion confuse the whole thing— they are totally unnecessary. And yet I suppose they are needed, until they are not. It all drops—drops completely when it's *seen*. No such thing as self-realization—unless seeing there is no self is it. No such thing as enlightenment or awakening, just looking and pointing. Wheeeeeeeeeeeee!

Ilona: Oh, I'm so happy for you! It's really that simple, and with *seeing*, seeking drops. Falling, sinking starts, and it has no end. Just different levels of intensity. I can see that the shift has happened. Can I ask you the final questions? If you are ready of course.

Yes, it's amazing to notice how this little misunderstanding causes so much confusion and suffering. I'm very happy to hear that you have the intention to help and point to others. It's a great gift to pass on. Much love to you!

Shanti: Thank you! I am ready. I will be off the grid from 5 p.m. tonight until late Sunday. Big hug.

Ilona: Sweet! Here they are.

Shanti: I will write Sunday night or Monday. Thank you.

Ilona: Looking forward to reading it. Have a great weekend, Love.

Shanti: Hi honey! It seems there was some effort to come here now and write this and isn't that just interesting—and to whom exactly?

1. Is there a separate entity "self," "me," "I," at all, anywhere, in any way, shape, or form? Was there ever?

No, no, no! Nope. Nada. And it is strange and a bit disorienting... but somehow familiar as well.

2. Explain in detail what the illusion of separate self is, when it starts, and how it works from your own experience. Describe it fully as you see it now.

"Shanti" began when there was an innocent kind of ownership. Yes, Shanti, "I" happened. It feels like an agreement, whatever that means. A sweet, precious, beautiful self yet completely meaningless. I don't know who she is but I am in love, no longer able to believe in her. I can love her deeply the same as one can love the story of Santa Claus and magic and unicorns. The self is like camouflage; a way of fitting in, making sense out of nonsense. The self is a collection of stories, ideas, images, sensations all sort of glued together in the attempt to give life meaning. Funny thing is, no self "over here," no self "over there."

3. How does it feel to see this? What is the difference from before you started this dialogue? Please report from the past few days.

The difference is a calm, balanced kind of experience. Shit still happens just as before but it isn't personal at all; even when it feels like it or appears to be, it isn't. Wobbly on my legs, a bit disorienting, and at the same time it seems like, yeah, well *duh!* And there's no doubt that it feels more, for lack of a better word, *real*. There seems to be a lot of settling going on, a falling away of stuff all on its own, or as if simple inquiry has come to life; life happening, life living.

4. What was the last bit that pushed you over? What made you look?

Whoa—I'm not sure. So much happened in a matter of a few days. One was a video of Elena [Nezhinsky] talking to someone; she said the sentence, "Can I think?" It hit me between the eyes and the falling really began. The next moment I e-mailed you. It had already begun. Then in our e-mails...there was a moment when you asked me, *Can you stop caring for your children?* That hit the mark. It was one of the last illusions too. Seeing the fear of losing them—somehow, once it was realized that I could not do it differently, fear left and seeing happened.

5. Do you decide, intend, choose, control events in life? Do you make anything happen? Give examples from your experience.

Ha ha! This was a fun one. It seems so convincing that someone or something is the master of the universe...and *no* choice, no intention, no deciding, no controlling. For example, I was eating dinner in a restaurant alone yesterday and I noticed, there was no one doing anything. Hand cut pizza, raised it to mouth, mouth opens, chewing, tasting, swallowing…so bizarre…no one doing it… no one at all.

I have also noticed that hand will move, sound will sound, and then thought will happen taking credit for the movement or sound… labeling it…none of what thoughts say it is true. Movement, seeing, sound, and even thoughts simply happen to no one, which is so strange to write.

6. Anything to add?

Thank you. I think I could write forever about all the stuff that has happened since seeing. Time has done a funny thing, as has space, and it's been interesting to notice when seeing gets somehow bent. Like when there is an argument with one of my children, they appear very big. I have to laugh out loud, it is so strange. I notice then that the patterns are dropping and this bending is part of that. When my children are giants or my husband a midget. I cannot play along any more. It is so silly. (Now this might all sound a bit crazy… but there you have it.) I felt wobbly but it feels more, no, not solid, but perhaps clearer with each moment. I am having very strange dreams as well, and energy seems to be endless even when tiredness is present. Thank you for you! And, how can I help? And, is there a place to talk about these weird things happening with others? Loving you.

Ilona: Dear Shanti, It was delightful to read your answers. I can see that you *see*. My heart is full of joy for you. Yes, there is a lot of settling in, a lot to clear up, a lot to recondition. And that takes time. This falling away of old beliefs happens whether you do work on that or just rest in being, the process takes care of itself. Sometimes it is intense, sometimes it's gentle, but there is no landing, only falling deeper and deeper into peace.

Could I put our conversation on my blog? I can use your name, or initial, or whatever name you are comfortable with. That way your process can be of help for someone else. It's like a giant wave rolling. Once it's on my blog I can ask other guides to see if they have any questions for you, and if all is clear, I invite you to the groups. There are many groups at Liberation Unleashed, and you too can start guiding.

If you would like to take any personal information out, no problem too. Much joy and love to you.

Shanti: Ilona! Share it, all of it. This one always has been an open book just really noticing there is nothing to hide, nothing personal, nothing to be careful about, and I appreciate you asking. I will answer any questions from anyone you would like me too. I might like to be a part of the groups and a guide. Thank you for your movement; much has been seen. Loving you. I have really loved our exchange and having you in my heart always. Thank you.

Ilona: I was walking and thinking of you. It's so sweet to connect. I too enjoyed our exchange and will put it on the blog today or tomorrow. It's really my pleasure to meet you and be part of your journey.

A few months later I received the following from Shanti.

What has changed for me? Before our meeting and discussions, so before the Gate, I had a lot of shifts, a lot of awakening moments, a lot of junk unraveled and was worked through, but it wasn't stable; it seemed to come and go, and when it went it was really ugly, dark, depression, sadness, meaninglessness, and not in a good way. There was desperation and wishes for death. There were a few more "veils" I was having a hard time seeing through; a big one was a fear of not loving my children if I really let go of everything. Through our conversations and your loving guidance, I was able to see those fears for what they were—nonsense. Since the Gate this understanding of

my experience as not personal and yet deeply personal has stabi-
lized. If despair shows up, it is not taken as personal or to have a
meaning about a "me." It comes and goes, and that which I am,
which I really cannot ever know, remains...always. I live as gratitude and move as joy. The ordinary *is* extraordinary and now I get
to *play*. Loving you and your movement in the world.

Suffering

Physical pain happens and is unavoidable, but mental pain, or suffering, is optional. Thoughts that tell the story about suffering *are* the suffering.

In my work with Liberation Unleashed, many people ask me to help them stop their suffering. People write me messages saying how much they suffer and how unbearable it is and how much they want to make it stop. I feel it's important to say something about suffering.

I know how bad it feels. I really do. I felt horrible many times, and all I wanted was to die. I used to cry and suffer. I used to feel this way periodically, and I saw life as being bits of sweet happiness in between feeling...well, the only word that describes it is "shitty." Life seemed unfair, harsh, and pointless.

I wasn't depressed, except for a few months after the process of deconstruction had started, but, in general, life sucked. In the background were constant feelings of "not enough," of not being good enough; I seemed to always be seeking relief, hiding, denying, pretending, and feeling rushed. I was looking for ways to improve my situation and constantly moving to the next self-help book or program that promised relief.

Some days were light and easy; some days were not. Expansion. Contraction. I did not like the contraction.

Nobody wants suffering. And yet it's here. What to do? How to get rid of it? Who can help? Hello!

If you are trapped in a vicious loop of darkness, you feel so hopeless and alone, and all feels pointless and meaningless. If you are looking for an Exit sign, here it is.

There Is No Sufferer

There is no sufferer. Not one at all. There is no one here at all. As it is with Santa Claus, the sufferer is imagined.

You think you are suffering, and this is the suffering. Yes, the story that your thoughts tell about suffering *is* the suffering. The story comes with emotions that you feel and resist. The story is a chain of thoughts about the "me" who is suffering. But let me ask you this: where is that "me" who claims to be the owner of feelings?

There is a story about a victim—a person who is tortured. Thoughts say that there is a victim.

But let's drop down from the head into the body for a bit.

How does suffering appear in the body? It's a sensation of contraction, of unwanted emotion. There is a sensation of tightness or emptiness like a dark, empty hole, but the description we use isn't the point. Bringing attention to sensing rather than thinking about suffering allows the tension to start dissolving. If you keep the focus on feeling, just letting it be there, letting it be okay, just watching the raw energy without naming it, the suffering starts to dissipate. Test this. For just one minute, allow the sensations to be here as they are, giving them space to unfold.

What is behind the tension?

Try This for Yourself   Is there a feeler?

Thought may say, *Yes, there is, it's* me.

But without thought, is there a "me"?

Is there anything separate in life from life?

Is there a *me-person* in the body?

If so, where is it?

Can you touch it?

Can you smell it, or taste it?

Can you hear it with ears or see it with eyes?

How do you know that it's there?

It seems to be in the head behind the eyes, it seems… But is it there?

How do you know for sure? Take a look.

Suffering and Acceptance

"Me" is not an entity living in the bag of skin, is not a soul having human experience, is not a separate avatar navigating through life, is not the narrator of the story; "me" is just not there. There is emptiness where a supposed being should be. And it's not a bad empty or a good empty; this emptiness is not the end to a little me. There is nothing there. Don't believe this? Then take a look.

The sufferer is not there, but there is a sensation and a story about suffering, right? And heavy, unbearable feelings too, yes? You may ask, "What's up with that?"

Try saying no to whatever is arising and yes to everything that is arising.

The sensations in the body, the contractions, only get stronger if you will them to go away. If you want to get rid of them, the sensations will feel even worse. The key is to *notice* resistance. Just notice that there is something that resists something. If you sense frustration and tension, locate them in the body. Feel them, let them be okay for one minute and twenty-three seconds. Watch them, make friends with them, and feel them fully, openly, and simply... Feel.

That's it.

Say yes to whatever is here. So be it. It is here already. It is here with and without your acceptance and approval. It's already here. It's okay to feel it.

Tension, when you notice and allow it to be here, starts melting. See this for yourself. Notice when resistance arises, and when you say yes to it, what happens?

If the feelings are so intense that they seem unbearable, it may help to learn the emotional freedom technique (see http://www .emofree.com/new-to-eft.html). Many people find it to be simple and effective, and there are plenty of books and free videos on YouTube offering instruction.

Yes, we view suffering as negative and unwanted. And it's okay. It's okay to want to drop it and feel at peace. It's okay to relax. You do not need to believe what thoughts say; you can directly focus on the sensations in the body instead. When you do so, there is no longer a need to try to stop the voice from talking. It's okay for it to be there. Just move the attention to the senses.

When all is welcomed, all will flow smoothly and sweetly.

When resistance shows up, and it will, just like breathing in and out, *notice* it.

Don't try to change anything, just notice.

Rinse and repeat.

Resistance and Frustration Are Our Friends

Right now it may be impossible to believe that resistance and frustration are your friends, but if you start noticing them, you will see where they lead. Resistance itself is not meant to be resisted, otherwise it locks into self-strengthening, repeating loops. Some say there is a path of least resistance, and when resistance melts, all that is left is surrender. This is the path of saying yes to whatever feeling, emotion, or sensation shows up.

> **Try This for Yourself** Notice frustration, watch how the mechanism works, and ask questions.
> What is behind it?
> What is here that feels threatened?
> What is here that wants to hold on?
> What needs to be protected?
> And from what, exactly?

Listening closely and noticing sensations in the body are key to releasing stuckness.

When one sees that there is nothing here that needs to be protected, the mechanism of frustration no longer gets triggered in the same way in certain situations. Don't expect happily ever after, because there is nothing permanent. Life is a movement of expansion and contraction. Things happen and will keep happening. The peace is here when there is no resistance to what already is.

So a start to the end of suffering is saying yes to it. It's okay to feel shitty. And it's okay to want to end it. It's okay to feel what is here now.

When you say yes, you may get really curious and interested to see for yourself where that sufferer is.

Try This for Yourself When a sensation comes up, look behind it. Is there someone who feels?

Can that someone be found in sense experience?

Or just in thinking?

Is that someone here now?

What is most important of all? To be kind to yourself. By saying *yes* to feelings and sensations, a door opens, and the habit of thinking about suffering starts losing its grip.

In short, it's not that you want to get rid of suffering, but rather to see for yourself, in your experience, that nothing exists where you think that "me," the sufferer, is.

Rowland

The looking process with Rowland took a couple of months. Our conversation was quite long, but I did not want to cut anything out. It was full-on looking and investigating. We covered many angles until all became clear. What amazes me is that even though Rowland started seeing a psychiatric nurse and getting a mental health assessment in the middle of the process, neither interfered or made the investigation difficult. He was looking with full focus and determination, and I was overjoyed for him.

Rowland: Hi Ilona, First of all, thank you so much for the awesome Liberation Unleashed website! I have been earnestly investigating the presence of the "I," seeing if it can be located. There seem to be one or two "sticky" areas.

How shall we start?

Ilona: Okay, so tell me what you are looking for?

How ready are you to see it?

What do you expect to see, experience, feel?

Rowland: Thanks, Ilona. I guess (if I am really honest) I am looking for some kind of "bliss" or "enlightened state" despite reading that there is no such thing! Certainly, the end to psychological, self-centered suffering which has dodged this body-mind for years (but is now starting to feel a bit lighter).

There is a bit of confusion as to inquiry. Should I be looking for the false, separate "I," or should I also be inquiring into presence/awareness itself (the big "I")? Maybe alternating between the two? I guess ultimately both are necessary. Seeing through the ego and noticing awareness as one's true, unchanging state—and getting really clear on this.

There is also a bit of conceptual confusion about presence/awareness which comes from reading too many books and writings by teachers. We are told that we are "not" the body or thoughts, we are the unchanging backdrop within which all arises. But also that body/world/thoughts are inseparable from this awareness! So, we are both unaffected by what arises and also intimately one with it? My mind spins in circles on this, not knowing where to focus! But I guess that is just what the mind does. There is a definite readiness to see it. I think I am expecting to see more clearly, and to feel "lighter" in terms of mental baggage. To see the "I" for what it is. Thank you, Ilona!

Ilona:

I guess (if I am really honest) I am looking for some kind of "bliss" or "enlightened state."

Nice. But this ain't about bliss or states. All states come and go and are not permanent. Some people have an awakening event and others just shrug—*Is that it?* It can be very subtle. There is no set way. The only way it happens is the right one for you, so bliss is not necessarily going to happen. You may rest this to the side for now. Seeing is pattern recognition, not a change of a state. It's a change of view.

Despite reading that there is no such thing! Certainly, the end to psychological, self-centered suffering which has dodged this body-mind for years (but is now starting to feel a bit lighter).

It is not the end of suffering. End of suffering happens when there are no more triggers left. And that is all conditioning. The whole structure that was built in years does not disappear instantly.

There is a bit of confusion as to inquiry. Should I be looking for the false, separate "I," or should I also be inquiring into presence/awareness itself (the big "I")? Maybe alternating between the two? I guess ultimately both are necessary. Seeing through the ego and noticing awareness as one's true, unchanging state—and getting really clear on this.

Okay, there is no big "I." Awareness is not "I." There is no ego as an entity in charge, there is nothing to get rid of, kill, or drop. Seeing through ego is realizing that there is no ego, it's just a label, a word used for communication about the behavioral patterns. Replace the word "ego" with the word "character" and it's not so negative anymore.

"Being" is not a noun, it's a verb, and there is nothing simpler or more natural than being.

Find the sense of being. Are you doing it?

Can you stop being for a second?

See what happens if you try.

There is a definite readiness to see it.

Oh great. That helps a lot.

I think I am expecting to see more clearly, and to feel "lighter" in terms of mental baggage. To see the "I" for what it is.

Yes, good one.

Okay, write to me if you are ready to leave all the above expectations behind and take a fresh look. Also, was anything in my answer triggering reactions? If so, what was it? Sending love.

Rowland: Thank you so much, Ilona. That was incredibly helpful! It made me realize how many mind-created expectations have still been in play.

Yes, I am certainly ready to leave these behind. This jumped out at me:

"Being" is not a noun, it's a verb, and there is nothing simpler or more natural than being.

Find the sense of being. Are you doing it?

Can you stop being for a second?

See what happens if you try.

There was a big *Yes!* to the simplicity of this! It is just "this" sense of being, right now. This aware-ing of sensations, sounds, thoughts, feelings, colors, and so forth. And, this awareness doesn't change, whilst everything that arises *in* it does. But they're not separate from it either. And this is something that thought is not going to grasp, is it? One of the things that I have struggled with in the past is the idea that the world arises in what I am, in awareness. So somehow awareness contains everything that is seen/heard/felt, and yet it nonetheless feels limited to the contours of this body; it feels like it is located inside "my" body. If that makes sense? Not sure how well I'm expressing myself here. But again, this is only an issue for thought. Pause the thought and where is the problem? Love and light!

Ilona: Nice, thank you for the answer. You say that it feels that awareness is contained in the body. Well, take a look to see if it's true.

When you hear a sound, is it heard in the body? Listen now.

When you smell something, is it felt in the body?

When you look at the distance, is the horizon in the body? Look, where is the line between here and there?

When you look down and see the legs, is awareness in the legs? Or in seeing? Take a look, can seeing be contained in the body?

What have you noticed?

Sending love.

Rowland: Thank you so much for your reply, Ilona. It had a powerful effect here. Sound feels neither inside nor outside. Perhaps
both. There doesn't seem to be an inside and an outside, on direct
evidence. These are thoughts.

When you smell something, is it felt in the body?

This is more subtle, but again, perhaps both inside and outside.

No, the horizon is not in the body and there is no way of demarcat-
ing "here" from "there." Or where seeing ends, and a "seen" object
begins. There is just "seeing." If I look back to see "where the one
who sees is," there is nobody immediately findable.

When I look at my legs, I just see varieties of color. There is also a
tactile sensation that, in direct evidence, is not necessarily "the
same as" the visual color—until thought comes in and says these
are all components of "leg," and all occur in the same place at the
same time. So awareness is not in the leg because the perception/
sensation of leg is a finite object. Does this make sense? "Leg" is
something I am aware "of." But it is not itself aware. It feels, as I
look, as if awareness is in the seeing. And then it feels that this
seeing is in the head. It does still feel quite strongly like "I" am
seeing from "my" head. But if I ask myself "Where is awareness?," it
is impossible to pin down. The sensations of "head," the thought "I,"
all occur within it. Then the thought arises: *This has to be "my"
body, as only "I" can feel it.*

Thank you again for this dialogue. It is so helpful! It is really cutting
away at ingrained assumptions. Love, R.

Ilona: Nice! Okay, so now investigate closely and see if there is a
boundary between inside and outside.

Try with eyes open and eyes closed. Is there inside and outside?

Is awareness contained?

In what? In the head?

Can you see your own head without a mirror?

Yes, you can only feel this body, not multiple bodies and not some other body. Does that mean you own this one?

Is there an owner at all?

Is it the body that experiences or is the body experienced?

Investigate and answer when ready. Sending love.

Rowland: Thank you, Ilona!

If I am really honest in terms of experience, and if I don't focus on thoughts, there is no evidence at all of a boundary. There is just sensation (the body) and perception (sounds, colors, smells) mediated by the body. Thought supplies the "me in here" and "you/it out there." Even the apparent boundary of the body is not that stable. If looked at closely, sensations are in constant flux; and with eyes closed, where does the sensation of "leg" end and "chair" begin? There is just undivided sensation. The sound of someone's voice that is arising at the moment (from the next room) is, oddly, arising "in me." Similarly, there is no evidence or possibility of awareness being contained, even in a head. Indeed, the sensations of "head," and even the notion of a "head," must arise within awareness. Awareness must be prior.

Yes, you can only feel this body, not multiple bodies and not some other body. Does that mean you own this one?

Is there an owner at all?

Thought powerfully insists that this is "my" body, but without thought, it is just sensation/perception. No owner; nothing personal. How is the sensation of "leg" more "mine" than the sensation of "chair" (when eyes are closed, going on direct evidence)? It is thought that supplies the narrative of "me" and "mine."

Is it the body that experiences or is the body experienced?

The body must be experienced. Awareness experiencing sensation/perception (and therefore simply experiencing itself)? A leg is not conscious, it is an object in consciousness like a tree or a tooth-brush. Or even a thought! What has become clear, as I have looked, is just how compelling thought is in constructing the "I." It takes the raw data of sensation and converts it into a heavy, ongoing narra-tive. How does one stop the I-thought from being so sticky and compelling? Thank you again, Ilona! Love, R.

Ilona: Good observations. Now look.

Are you awareness?

Is it personal?

Is awareness prior to, or is it arising together with, the objects that it is being aware of?

Can it be separated?

In experience now, listen to sound; is there anything there besides what is heard?

It is thought that supplies the narrative of "me" and "mine." Yes, "owner" is an assumption.

How does one stop the I-thought from being so sticky and compelling?

See it as empty and nothing sticks to it anymore.

What does the word "I" point to?

Here are some questions for you to sit with. Much love back.

Rowland: Thank you so much, Ilona! I have been sitting with your questions, reflecting on them.

Without the narrative of thought, there is no sense in which aware-ness could be called "personal." It is not "mine." Ideas like "mine" arise and fall within it. It just *is*.

Also: if it were "personal," this would require the dualism of "other persons"; and again, on present evidence, there are no "other persons." (This was quite a shock when it first hit me! It left me feeling strangely lonely but again, this is only because a thought had slipped in and was being believed. *I am alone*—but is there actually an "I" to be lonely?)

"Other people" are only present awareness: they cannot be separated from what is aware right now. Awareness therefore cannot be separated, although I also intuit that it cannot be affected: it is both changeless and the substance of change at the same time (if this makes sense?). It is aware of (say) a sound, noticing it come and go; and it also *is* that sound in its entirety. Again, I hope I am expressing this clearly! So, I think it is both prior to experience, and also one with experience. It has to be prior/changeless in order to register change; but it is not in any way apart from change, either. When a sound is heard, there is just the hearing, no "hearer," no "sound," in fact. Just the hearing.

See it as empty and nothing sticks to it anymore.

What does the word "I" point to?

When this question is asked, there is just silence. Thought might then come in and make suggestions, but it can only refer to other thoughts. Even "this body" or "this mind" or "these memories" are other thoughts. Memory, however, does seem to be sticky and compelling here: it weaves a seemingly strong narrative of "me" going back in time. But perhaps the question is: To whom do memories refer? To which individual? Thank you again, your e-mails are so helpful! Love, R.

Ilona: Great stuff, you are on the right track.

Watch the YouTube video of Alan Watts talking about the "boat analogy" [see the video at https://www.youtube.com/watch?v= G4j6cUwCRmI]; it's about time. This is actually a great picture of how past appears to be. Then, contemplate what you notice now when looking at a memory of a past event.

Find the feeling of being, aliveness, am-ness. Just sit and feel for a bit.

Can you tell if there is *a* being or just *being*?

Is life happening *to a* being or *as* being?

What do you notice?

When you look at nature and how all moves interdependently, is that movement outside of you? Is there a "you"?

Sending love.

Rowland: Thank you, Ilona! The video was very clear.

Contemplate what you notice now when looking at a memory of a past event.

Memories of past events only ever arise now, in this moment. A memory only seems to refer to another thought or memory. Where is the "me" whom memories describe? Where is the "me" who "has" a past? If I look for one, I can't find one. Memories arise like anything else: sounds, sights, sensations, perceptions. Only another thought makes them personal, and then they become the memories of a "me." This brings a lightness. Although the I-thought still feels quite strong, it has definitely loosened a bit. There is just what is happening now, naturally, spontaneously. Awareness does not have the anxious preoccupation with time that the mind has, moving compulsively into past and future; in fact, it *cannot* move into past or future! It is just here, now, naturally and effortlessly aware. There is such a simplicity to this. I think I need to sit with it a bit more, too.

Find the feeling of being, aliveness, am-ness. Just sit and feel for a bit.

Can you tell if there is a *being or just* being?

Without the thought *This is happening to me, this is my body*, there is just being. There is physical sensation (hands on a keyboard); visual sensation (colors on and around a screen); the sound of a dog barking, of my hands typing; the sensation of thoughts arising and falling. All of this is changing, moment by moment. And there is something here that is noticing this change, and is not the change. But equally, it is not in any way apart from the change (Does that make sense?). Perhaps it is clearer to say that arisings depend on awareness and cannot be separated from awareness; but that awareness does not depend on arisings (as in deep sleep). It is ultimately unaffected by them. For a moment there was frustration here, too: an irritation with the body and thought, and a desire to get away from them, as if they are obstacles to seeing clearly. But who is irritated or frustrated? In fact, who needs to see clearly? Is seeing clearly not already naturally, spontaneously happening, and just being missed?

Is life happening to a being or as being?

What do you notice?

Life is happening as being, again, unless there is an investment in self-referential thought. It is happening "to a being" if there is a separate "being"—a person doing the being, acting apart from the rest of life. But where is this separate being "doing" the being?

When you look at nature and how all moves interdependently, is that movement outside of you? Is there a "you"?

Nothing is outside being-awareness, the colors/sounds/smells/tactile information/movement of nature cannot be separated from what is presently aware here, even though (paradoxically) what is presently aware itself does not move. The green color of a leaf, for example: How could this be separated from the seeing of it? Could it exist outside the seeing of it? The sound of a bee, or rain drumming on the roof, can these experiences be separated from the hearing of them? It can be quite shocking (in a good way) to see how assumptions operate. For example, the idea that when I leave my house to go to work, the house continues to exist independently. Where is the evidence for this? Where is the evidence that the house exists away from or apart from this present awareness? There is almost a feeling that awareness "composes" an apparent world, moment by moment, that the "world" is only the present (immediate) contents of consciousness. So, for example: I can presently see the computer, books, a cup, the wall in front of me; there is the sensation of a chair; there is the sound of my cat's claws. Where is the evidence that there is anything else? For example; a town, another country, a world in which other things are happening, even a universe? This makes me feel strangely lonely—there is just this awareness, nothing and nobody else—but, who is lonely? Awareness may be utterly alone (all-one), but is it lonely? Thank you again, Ilona. Love, R.

Ilona: What is awareness?

Some kind of lone witness?

Or is witnessing too just happening, done by no one?

Is awareness a container in which all arises?

Keep digging.

Rowland: Thank you, Ilona! I have been sitting with and investigating the questions above; here are my reflections.

If a thought arises, say, the thought *I am hungry*, it is seen or witnessed. But, if the seer or witness is looked for, there is nobody there. If the thought *It's me that sees the thought* arises, then who witnesses this thought? Again: there is just emptiness. A "me" cannot be located that is not a transient thought, that is not an object that comes and goes. Awareness cannot be a container, as this would suggest boundaries or limits and these are not present, looking now in direct evidence. A container would also suggest a divide between awareness and its contents (like thoughts and perceptions) but again, this does not seem true to experience. Can a thought be separated from the awareness that notices it? What could a thought be outside of awareness? Where would "thought" end and "awareness of thought" begin? It would be impossible to mark any kind of division. Having said this, there does also seem to be a subtle difference: awareness itself is changeless, and therefore perceives change, so perhaps it is also prior to experience? If awareness itself was subject to change, the arising and falling of a thought would not be seen. And although a thought cannot be separated from aware presence, it is not itself aware. Nor is a sensation in a leg or arm.

Ilona: This made me smile. You cannot think your way out of this. Take a closer look.

Wait for a thought, notice its arrival and departure. See how it's a tiny blink and how it is in itself empty. Thought + thought + thought becomes an expression, description, which in itself is empty. Now try this: get something tasty and experience the taste. Just feel it for a minute.

Focus on the sensation of tasting. What is it that does the tasting behind the sensation?

Is there anything behind?

Then for another minute describe that taste, describe in words what was felt. How similar or different are the experience and the description of it?

What do you notice here?

Do the same with smell. Take something and experience it, then describe in words.

Now try to describe awareness, just as you see it. What do you notice?

Sending love.

Rowland: Thank you, Ilona, for reminding me of the way thought tries to get a "grasp" on all of this! I think quite a bit of suffering and frustration come from this, and then trying to square what one teacher says with what another says, and then thought is spinning, and saying, *I'm never going to get this!* The mind is always trying to conceptualize; it is always looking for satisfaction, which it will never get. Perhaps it is also trying not to confront the fact of its own nonexistence!

Wait for a thought, notice its arrival and departure. See how it's a tiny blink and how it is in itself empty.

Yes, this is clear: the thought "I" just arose, and left. But the space remains unaffected.

Now try this: get something tasty and experience the taste. Just feel it for a minute.

Focus on the sensation of tasting. What is it that does the tasting behind the sensation?

Is there anything behind?

There is no one who does the tasting—just the sensation of taste, immediate and present. The thought *I am tasting this* comes up automatically but then passes, and the taste remains.

Then for another minute describe that taste, describe in words what was felt. How similar or different are the experience and the description of it?

What do you notice here?

Initially I found it quite hard describing taste in words, and what struck me was the difference (total difference) between description and actual experience! What does the word "sweet" actually have in common with the sensation of "sweetness"?

Do the same with smell. Take something and experience it, then describe in words.

The same again. The description of "smell," and the experience of it: almost no relation!

Now try to describe awareness, just as you see it. What do you notice?

One thing that has struck me while doing this investigation is how any verbal description doesn't come close to actual experience. And yet we believe so strongly that words tell us what is "real." Awareness feels like a kind of space in which everything is coming and going, which can't be separated from those comings and goings but is not affected by them (even though it feels like it is). It is silent, alert, open, nonjudgmental. It doesn't have any issues or preferences regarding any sensations that might come up.

For example, quite a lot of anxiety has been coming up over the past few days (I have suffered from panic, depression, and OCD for quite a few years). The mind constructs a horrible story around the sensations of fear, but awareness, if I look now, is just aware of what is happening. It is not wishing anything away.

Thank you, Ilona! I hope this e-mail finds you well and enjoying the sunshine. Love, R.

Ilona: Good work, Rowland! Let's dig deeper. There is an exercise on my blog called "Labels" [see page 76 in this book]; do the exercise and write to me what you noticed. There is also an article on language [see "The Trick of Language" on page 73 of this book] in the articles section; read that too. So today, investigate how language works and report when ready. Much love.

Rowland: Thank you so much for that exercise, Ilona, really powerful and revealing! I found that writing without the "I"/"me" was less tense, no need to refer experience to an "I." It felt lighter, more free. I also noticed how tempting it was to bring in an "I," and how much the mind resisted this! Several times I had to catch myself when about to write "I hear" and so forth. The mind really wanted to own this. I feel at the moment like the mind really, really does not want to hear that it (the "I") does not exist, and is afraid. It feels uncomfortable, almost, if it is not thinking and referring experience back to an "I," and it will try anything to survive! Here is what I wrote (sorry, it's probably extremely boring).

With "me"/"I":

> I am sitting in my chair at work. I am listening to the sounds outside: voices, cars, the hum of traffic, doors closing in the

corridor. I am typing—I can feel the sensation of my fingers on the keys of the keyboard, I can see the colors of the keyboard and computer, I can hear the sounds of the typing as my fingers move over the keyboard.

Without "me"/"I":

Sitting in the chair. Sensation of hardness against the feet. Pausing and hearing sounds outside. There are voices and doors opening and closing. Pausing again. Fingers moving over keyboard, sensation of hardness and cold. Pause. Hearing police siren outside. Pause, wondering what to write.

Thank you again, Ilona! Hope you are enjoying the bright summer sunshine. Love, R.

Ilona: Hi Rowland. Thanks for your reply. I see you missed the point of the second part of the exercise, slightly. The instruction was to write all in verbs, without subject doing action, just description of action happening. Try again, see if you notice a difference. Just go a little bit deeper into expressing experiencing through verbs; you had that in the beginning, but then it slipped. Use "ing" with words, like "feeling," "hearing." See if you notice more continuity, movement.

Does the description of what is happening influence what is happening? If so, what and how? Does it matter if you add "I" and "me" to the description, does that make "I" and "me" a doer?

Is there a doer?

Sending love.

Rowland: Thank you, Ilona. Sorry about the misunderstanding! I have just repeated the exercise (below is what I wrote). I found it very effective; it made me realize what a load of anxiety the belief in the "I" generates!

Does the description of what is happening influence what is happening? If so, what and how? Does it matter if you add "I" and "me" to the description, does that make "I" and "me" a doer?

No, the description does not influence what is happening, there are sounds/sights/sensations which are immediate. The description felt is completely secondary. With "I" and "me" added in, it felt heavier, with a weight of responsibility, as if "I" am doing the hearing, feeling, seeing, pausing, thinking, turning. If I look now, "I" cannot be the doer, however strong the conditioning might be, "I" is a thought that comes and goes. It seems to be the doer, but it cannot be. There is no real difference between the thoughts "I" or "Rowland" or "me" and the thoughts "broccoli" or "spirituality" or "chakra" or "rhubarb." If I ask, "To what does the thought 'I' refer?" I can't find anything. Just sensations and a kind of emptiness. It occurred to me that the link between the I-thought and the sensations of "body" is just an assumption.

Is there a doer?

It feels like there is one, but I can't find one. The I-thought certainly cannot be the doer. A "doer" of thought can't be found either.

Here is what I wrote the second time:

> Sitting in chair, looking at screen, noticing letters, waiting for thought to arise, listening to voices outside, listening to doors opening and closing, feeling breath rising and falling, waiting for thought, listening to traffic, listening to clock ticking, feeling fingers on keyboard.

Thanks so much, Ilona! Love, R.

Ilona: Great observations! I see you are looking right at it. Yes, there seems to be a doer, but is there one? Maybe there is just doing happening? Walking, breathing, showering, raining, just happening. And it's only a label that assumes an object does the action. Take a look at how language creates the illusion. It's a good idea at this point to get out in natural surroundings and observe the totality of movement. While sitting and walking, watch how all is wiggling, all is moving interdependently, and that includes thinking and feeling, sensing with senses.

Is there anything that is separate from everything else?

Is there a line that divides me from everything else, or is it just a thought, an assumption?

Is there an inside and an outside?

Is there an owner of the body?

An owner of life?

How about a tree, is there an owner-tree inside that tree?

There are some questions for you to play with. Write to me once you have done this exercise. Looking forward to hearing from you. Much love.

Rowland: Thank you, Ilona! I really do appreciate your help and guidance. Nothing is separate except in thought, it is a play of sensations appearing in present awareness. Lots of movement and change, appearing in what doesn't change, and not separate from that. And it is all happening presently, and presently, and presently. As I watched (a bee on a flower, the wind passing through a tree, horses eating grass, clouds moving in the sky), what hit me was a sense of lightness in nature. Everything just freely moving, but not "as" anything particular. A horse is not going around thinking, *I am a horse, but I'm not a tree or a bee.* It is just freely, brightly being. This is not to say that nature is always "nice" or "good"; it is beyond such categories, and much simpler. It is just what is happening, without judgement. Whether a beautiful flower opening to the sun, or a dying bird, or a cloud fading, or a spider catching and eating a struggling fly. Just what is happening. Any judgement on this is an imposition of the mind.

Is there an inside and an outside?

Again, it's only thought that divides. There is no inside or outside, except in thought. No "me watching something separate called nature." The body might feel separate, but does it? Is it? It is just the arising and falling of a cluster of sensations. These are not boundaries unless they are conceptualized. There is the sensation of a leg, and the visual sensation of a flower, both sensations appearing equally in, and equally "close" to, awareness.

Is there an owner of the body?

An owner of life?

How about a tree, is there an owner-tree inside that tree?

There seems to be an "owner" of the body, but if I look now I can't find one. These hands are moving over the keyboard without the guidance of thought or any "doing" entity. Thoughts are appearing, and then going onto the screen, but where are these thoughts coming from? There is also no thought going into the movement of my hands. Things are happening quite spontaneously. It is conditioning, which does feel very strong, that insists otherwise. It still feels as if there is an entity inside my head, but again, as I pause now and look, I can't find one. I can't even find a head! Thought then says: *Maybe there is one, but it can't be found.* But this is just thought spinning away to keep itself in the illusory driving seat. It feels like it doesn't want to give up!

Love, R.

Ilona: Hi Rowland. Nice work. You are getting close.

Now look:

Can the body feel separate?

Is it the body that experiences or is the body experienced?

Is there an experiencer at all?

If you look at perceiver/perceiving/perceived, is there a gap?

Is there a perceiver to which perception is happening?

Test it with each sense and write what you notice.

Sending love.

Rowland: Thanks so much, Ilona. The sensations of the body are certainly experienced; but I can't say with any certainty that the body itself experiences. Sensations are an object, they are experienced—like the sounds I can currently hear (cars, voices, sound of keys typing). The body just "feels" personal; it "feels" like it is experiencing because of years of conditioning. If I ask who is experiencing sensations, I can't find anyone. I can't find an experiencer, just thoughts that come up and hypnotically assert themselves as an "I." Sometimes thoughts say: *There is an "I," but it just can't be seen, because it is what I am.* But where is the evidence for this? It feels like thought is pulling out all the stops, really fighting dirty! There is no findable perceiver, just perception being noticed.

Sound is registering here right now…tactile sensation…taste…smell…and the thought "I" or "me" or "Rowland" is equally being noticed by something…there are no gaps…just hearing, and so on.

There has been quite a bit of frustration here over the past couple of days. Thought has been coming up powerfully: *I will never get this, I am unworthy of this.* I seem to recognize this on some level, and yet on another level, moment to moment, the I/me/Rowland-thought still seems to be *so* strong and believable, still seems to take hold. It feels like it can be seen through momentarily. I can see the thought *I* right now, come and go, and yet seconds later it comes back and hooks me. But where is the *me* who gets hooked? Again, nothing can be found.

Thank you again for guiding me on this journey, Ilona!

Love, R.

Ilona:

If I ask who is experiencing sensations, I can't find anyone.

The "who" question assumes an entity. There isn't one. That's how the answer is blank.

The body seems to feel that it is the experiencer because of a belief, unquestioned assumption, and yes, years of conditioning.

Take a look: Is there an "owner" of the body?

Thought can say many things. It can say that I am a pink panther. But the content of thought is a description, label, fiction, not actuality. There is an "I," there isn't an "I"; it's just thoughts. The trick is to look where thoughts point to, where words make you look. Like the analogy of the finger pointing to the moon, words are fingers, the moon is experience.

It feels like it can be seen through momentarily. I can see the thought I right now, come and go, and yet seconds later it comes back and hooks me. But where is the me *who gets hooked? Again, nothing can be found.*

Oh yeah, there is a stage of going in and out, it will pass. Don't try to understand, just watch it happening and let it go. Focus on experience rather than the story and keep looking, you are getting close.

Is there anything you expect or hope to happen?

If so, what?

Love back to you!

Rowland:

Take a look: Is there an "owner" of the body?

When I look for one, I can't find one. Sensations, feelings, perceptions, happening now. Thought bubbling under with a *But...*trying to assert that there is an owner somewhere. *Yes...but...* That familiar voice in the head. So an owner of experience can't be found, just experience. Yet, there is still this strong sense of an owner, somewhere.

Is there anything you expect or hope to happen?

If so, what?

It's strange that even though there is this subtle loosening, an almost imperceptible link of pinpricks of light, it doesn't *feel* like I am getting close. But, that is thought again perhaps, getting back to its old tricks. I decided this morning to have a fresh look at this "sense of self" that seems to persist, and to get rid of any non-dual language I might be using. I think maybe I have gotten too comfortable with this, having read so many non-dual books (and having bought the mug and t-shirt!). So, just authentic, honest, moment-by-moment writing of what is being seen. Just that. Here is what I wrote down. I hope it sort of makes sense, as I wrote fast, apart from pausing to look.

> Why does this sense of self persist so strongly? It feels odd: on the one hand, I definitely can't locate a separate self. When I have a look, all I can find is thoughts/feelings/sensations and something that notices these. Nothing else. Nothing that stays the same, nothing that isn't in a constant process of change, apart from the noticing, which is constant. When I have another look now, what I think is that keeping the sense of self going is still belief in thought. It is the thoughts that are like a "stuck record" in my head, particularly memory thoughts. These still draw me in and make me think I am a "me" unfolding in time. They seem very compelling. They are often painful memories that replay, sometimes from years ago. They tell me things like, *I am unworthy* or *I am bad.* They tell me I am not "spiritual" enough, whatever that means. These are the kind of thoughts which I have suffered from even since childhood, self-punishing thoughts.
>
> I'm going to have a good head-on look at this now. No non-dual language either! Where is the one to whom memories

apply? What can be found? To whom do memories belong? What can actually be found when these questions are asked?

I find sensations, perceptions (sound of the oven, sound of cooking, sound of my pen on paper), thoughts. I find other sensations that might be called feelings. (Sensations in chest and stomach right now—they're difficult to label because they keep moving about. The main feeling, though, is a little hint of freedom/joy, as not much is being found.)

Is there anyone here that memory describes, or belongs to? Anyone at all?

Can't find anyone again.

Memories (like all thoughts) come and go in impersonal space (oops, that sounds a bit non-dual, but you know what I mean). They don't refer to anything real. The past is not present; a memory is a thought referring to another thought. What is real are the thoughts themselves. All this is coming up spontaneously, thoughts/feelings/sensations. Stuff coming up! Memories are no more "mine" than the sound of the oven is mine. Why? There is equal awareness of both. Something notices the memory-thought, I made a cup of coffee five minutes ago. Something notices the sound of the oven. That something is not any closer to the thoughts than it is to the sound of the oven, even though those thoughts will say otherwise. Memory thoughts are not mine. They don't describe a me! How could they? Where is the me described in memory? Nothing there. Nada. Silence.

While looking above, I noticed that thought seemingly wants to interrupt, as if there is a fear of being found out. There is a sense of something bad/rotten/sinful at the core that has been there since childhood. But where is this one who is bad/ rotten/sinful? Does he actually exist? Scary place to look. Looking. Thoughts/sensations. Can't find him, again!

Sorry to write so much above! But it helped having a good, hard, honest look. It felt good to really look for the person who is presumed to exist. I felt good at the end of it, a bit lighter. I think what I need to do (I?) is to keep digging, keep looking, be persistent, as the so-called "person" quickly seems to solidify and become heavy again. As I am writing this, it feels strongly like Rowland is writing it again. So I just need to keep digging, questioning, looking. Rowland comes back in so quickly. The empty something feels like it is wispy and fragile, when I know it's not because it's actually what's real.

Thank you, Ilona! My gratitude to you is more than I can express. I need to ignore those thoughts that tell me *I will never get this.*

Love, R.

Ilona:

Yet, there is still this strong sense of an owner, somewhere.

Sense of an owner or an unquestioned assumption that there must be an owner.

Can you find an owner of sensations?

Test with each sense. Is there an owner of heard sounds?

Why does this sense of self persist so strongly? It feels odd: on the one hand, I definitely can't locate a separate self. When I have a look, all I can find is thoughts/feelings/sensations and something that notices these. Nothing else. Nothing that stays the same, nothing that isn't in a constant process of change, apart from the noticing, which is constant.

Yes, noticing awareness is always present, and its content, which is movement, is like a kaleidoscopic ever-changing movie of sensation, thoughts, and feelings.

Look more closely: Is there something that notices, and is what is noticed one and the same? Is there a gap?

When I have another look now, what I think is that keeping the sense of self going is still belief in thought. It is the thoughts that are like a "stuck record" in my head, particularly memory thoughts. These still draw me in, make me think I am a "me" unfolding in time. They seem very compelling.

Yes, thought says there is a sense of self. Take a look with senses.

Is there a sense of self in seeing, hearing, tasting?

Where and when does the sense of self arise exactly?

They are often painful memories that replay, sometimes from years ago. They tell me things like, I am unworthy or I am bad. They tell me I am not "spiritual" enough, whatever that means. These are the kind of thoughts which I have suffered from even since childhood, self-punishing thoughts.

Thoughts of judgement affect how we feel, but are they true?

Is it true that you are unworthy? Is it true that there is someone here to be unworthy?

How is unworthiness felt?

What is behind the sensations?

Is there a feeler of sensations to which sensations happen?

Memories (like all thoughts) come and go in impersonal space (oops, that sounds a bit non-dual, but you know what I mean). They don't refer to anything real. The past is not present; a memory is a thought referring to another thought. What is real are the thoughts themselves.

Thoughts are here to be noticed, not to be believed.

All this is coming up spontaneously, thoughts/feelings/sensations. Stuff coming up!

Yes. All is happening in the present—sensations, thoughts, feelings.

Is there a center to which they all happen?

While looking above, I noticed that thought seemingly wants to interrupt, as if there is a fear of being found out. There is a sense of something bad/ rotten/sinful at the core that has been there since childhood.

Good one: Examine that closer, what is there that feels rotten? What is behind it?

Yes, yes, great stuff. Keep looking. And when Rowland comes back, check to see if that is not just a thought too, appearing effortlessly.

Rowland: Thank you so much, Ilona! I have had an interesting couple of days. On Sunday night, lying in bed, I was overcome by a feeling of terror as I lay there. A sense of profound disorientation, of not being able to find Rowland, of not being separate from anything (including the sensations of the bed I was lying on). Then yesterday morning, walking to the bus stop on the way to work, I was again seized by an intense fear, almost a panic attack. The closest I can describe was that it was like a kind of agoraphobia, like I had no boundaries, *I was everywhere and everything* at the same time: the trees I was seeing, the feel of the road beneath my feet, the clouds in the sky, the sound of the cars, all were as much *me* as the sensations of the body—sensations which hardly seemed to be there for a period. I felt dispersed, dissolved, and like I would lose my mind! Then, as I sat on the bus, the fear slowly dissolved.

While I was in this fearful state and unable to locate Rowland, there was equally no concern at all about all Rowland's apparent worries and problems and stories! They seemed distant. I am deliberately not dwelling on this experience, though, as it is just an experience. Something similar happened about a couple of months ago: walking up the stairs to the bathroom, I was overwhelmed by fear at not being able to locate Rowland; there was a sense of panicking, desperately trying to reassert him. But looking now, it is not that I am afraid. Where is the "I" that is afraid? Having a look now.

Fear is a sensation/feeling that is experienced like any other. It is experienced in the same way as the sound of the clock ticking, or the feel of the floor beneath my feet right now. It feels like something is "more" aware of feeling than sound but is that actually true right now? It only seems that way because we have been conditioned to believe that feelings arise in something called "my personal body." This itself is just sensations coming up now. What notices these sensations (called "body"), these feelings, these thoughts about experience, the sound of the clock? All really sensations, even thoughts. Looking now and nothing there but a sense of something wide and transparent and peaceful which can't be found.

Sense of an owner or an unquestioned assumption that there must be an owner.

Can you find an owner of sensations?

Test with each sense. Is there an owner of heard sounds?

Looking for an owner of heard sounds and can't find anything. There is just the sound of the clock ticking, footsteps, and so forth— just the hearing which is totally effortless. Is there anyone making hearing happen? Looking. No. Thought might say that "I" am "hearing," but that is not true. How can a thought hear?

Can't find an owner of seeing, either. There is just automatic seeing that can't be stopped or started. If I close my eyes, there is still seeing. Seeing is happening. Can the thoughts "I" or "Rowland" see? No. Can't find a taster, can't find a smeller. What occurs to me is that only another thought links the I-thought to different sensations, the I-thought is itself a sensation. All just sensations appearing and disappearing. Thought, feeling, sound, sight.

Is there anything you expect or hope to happen?

If so, what?

If I am really honest, there is still a longing for peace and harmony, and an end to psychological suffering, and maybe the occasional blissful experience.

Look more closely: Is there something that notices, and is what is noticed one and the same? Is there a gap?

Yes, thought says there is a sense of self. Take a look with senses.

Is there a sense of self in seeing, hearing, tasting?

Where and when does the sense of self arises exactly?

There is no sense of self in seeing, hearing, tasting. There is just seeing, hearing, tasting, the sound of traffic, fingers tapping away, the feel of the keyboard, the colors on the screen. Where is the "I" in all of this? It is only in thought that a sense of self arises. Nowhere else. The sense of "my body" still feels strong and persistent. It still feels like it "houses" awareness, even though it is seen that sensations are noticed by something, including sensations of "my body." Perhaps a bit more looking is needed here.

Thoughts of judgement affect how we feel, but are they true?

Is it true that you are unworthy? Is it true that there is someone here to be unworthy?

How is unworthiness felt?

What is behind the sensations?

Is there a feeler of sensations to which sensations happen?

Looking behind the sensations, behind seeing and hearing, and can't find anything. Just hearing and seeing, and something noticing the sounds and sights. It feels like there is a something that feels "inside a body" but that body is just sensations right now. It doesn't even have an inside. Sensations are just happening, including the sensations labeled "my body." If I look closely, these "body" sensations are even changing every second (the mind makes the body into something solid and stable). There are bits of my body that aren't even being felt right now.

Yes. All is happening in the present—sensations, thoughts, feelings.

Is there a center to which they all happen?

Can't find one! It feels like there is one, but this is only an assumption. Looking at hearing alone right now, it is unclear if "I" am over where the sounds "are," or whether I am "here," where the sounds are seemingly being heard. Feeling wide and spread out.

Yes, yes, great stuff. Keep looking. And when Rowland comes back, check to see if that is not just a thought too, appearing effortlessly.

Yes, will keep noticing and checking. Rowland feels heavy again in the moment, but is he here? All that is found are sounds, sensations, sights, and thoughts. (*Yes, Rowland is here*) and something noticing all this that seems to be inside a body still. Always thoughts that cause the problems, cheeky blighters! Thank you so much, Ilona! There is a subtle loosening, although I need to keep looking, looking, looking.

Love, R.

Ilona: Thank you for sharing your experience. When it happens next time, see if you can welcome that fear when it is there and allow it to pass. This oneness that was seen is not here to scare you, it's seeing that there are no boundaries, all is one, no separation.

If I am really honest, there is still a longing for peace and harmony, and an end to psychological suffering, and maybe the occasional blissful experience.

Peace is always here, it's only the longing for peace that is covering it up. Look right now, underneath the thinking, behind experience, can you feel this peace? It's not a state that comes and goes, but rather a background to that which comes and goes. If the mind wants peace, ask it, literally, what is in the way of feeling peace now. See what it is that the mind wants the most, then check if that wanting is the one thing that creates tension.

Also, examine this closely: what is the sensation that you call "Rowland"?

You say that sensations are noticed by something. That something is an assumption too. There is noticing happening, being aware, focusing on experiences, no subject is doing any of it, it's just simply happening.

When there is a feeling that Rowland is back, see what is really happening that is labeled "Rowland."

Here is something special for you, Bahiya Sutra [see http://awaken ingtoreality.blogspot.sg/2008/01/ajahn-amaro-on-non-duality-and .html]. Write to me what you notice after spending time with it.

> *In the seen, there is only the seen,*
> *in the heard, there is only the heard,*
> *in the sensed, there is only the sensed,*
> *in the cognized, there is only the cognized.*
> *Thus you should see that*
> *indeed there is no thing here;*
> *this, Bahiya, is how you should train yourself.*
> *Since, Bahiya, there is for you*
> *in the seen, only the seen,*
> *in the heard, only the heard,*
> *in the sensed, only the sensed,*
> *in the cognized, only the cognized,*
> *and you see that there is no thing here,*
> *you will therefore see that*
> *indeed there is no thing there.*
> *As you see that there is no thing there,*

you will see that
you are therefore located neither in the world of this,
nor in the world of that,
nor in any place
between the two.
This alone is the end of suffering.

Much love.

Rowland: Thank you so much, Ilona, for all your patience. Will spend a couple of days looking with your e-mail, reflecting on those beautiful lines, and get back to you. Love, R.

Rowland: I hope this e-mail finds you well. Below is my latest response.

As I look, it is clear that anything that is covering up the peace is thought-based. It is not the thoughts themselves that create distur-bance, as much as belief in those thoughts. It is believing that the I-thought points to something real. It feels like this needs to be really, really clearly seen here. I have been writing a lot in my journal over the past couple of days, and noticing especially when "Rowland" comes up most strongly. Some jealousy arose in me yesterday in rela-tion to a work colleague, which was interesting: almost immediately there was a sense of anger and guilt, as if this is not a "spiritual" emotion and that I should not be feeling it! But I had a good look at the one who was feeling jealous and couldn't find him. Just thoughts/feelings/sensations coming and going. The thoughts/feelings per-sisted quite strongly, but I couldn't find a central "I" to direct them. So nobody to take ownership. Nobody to say, "I am jealous"—but equally, nobody to say, "I shouldn't feel jealous." All these things just happening, just arising!

You say that sensations are noticed by something. That something is an assumption too. There is noticing happening, being aware, focusing on experiences, no subject is doing any of it, it's just simply happening.

Yes, I think there is a tendency here to turn awareness into another object or person. When direct experience is looked at, there is nobody "behind" thoughts/feelings/perceptions. Nobody can be found, even though this feels fleeting at times. There is a noticing of what comes and goes, a presence (Is this the right word?) that is not changing, that is aware of change: that is not judging, that is always present. It is the sense of just being. It is always here. The I-thought comes and goes in it. Sensations of the body come and go in it. Sounds and sights come and go in it.

The Bahiya Sutra is very powerful, and I will keep working with it. What has come up with it has been the reminder that there is just this, *just* the hearing, the seeing, the touching, the thinking—all without an entity behind them. Everything just coming up now, now, now. There is certainly a "lightening" of the "Rowland" burden at the moment, a subtle sense of ease filtering in, even in the midst of a stressful teaching job. Just observing that even during crazy lessons, there are just sounds/sights/perceptions/thoughts coming and going. There is no "me" controlling them.

This feels like it is getting clearer but that I need to keep digging for it to become clearer still. It doesn't quite feel yet like a "lived reality," if you know what I mean. I have found writing/journaling very helpful by getting it all on paper. Looking on paper. I think it is important for me to stick with the simplicity of this. Thought here has such a tendency to conceptualize, to compare what one teacher says with another (about awareness, consciousness, and so forth), and it gets snared in loops of confused, anxious thinking! If I pause thought now, how complicated is any of this? How much does natural being need to "figure out"? It doesn't, it feels like it just needs to settle in gently with a recognition of what is real. Thank you, as ever, Ilona, for all your compassion, guidance, and amazing patience! I really enjoyed your interview with the Wizard. [The interview is available at http://podcast.liberationunleashed.com/2011/12/ilona-wizard-radio-show.] Love and light.

Ilona: Hey Rowland. Thank you for answers! Yes, you are staring right at it. Now do the math.

Is there a separate "self," "I," or "me" at all, in any shape or form?

Was there ever?

How does it feel to answer as you answer?

Much love.

Rowland: Thank you, as ever, for the amazing gift of your expression, Ilona! At the moment I feel rather confused, but will just write as it comes, without filters. On the one hand, it feels like I can't find a separate self if I look for it. I can only find thoughts/feelings and I-thought sensations; yet, on the other hand, there still seems to be that self operating with a kind of "heaviness," but I'm not sure how or where. I'm not sure if thought is simply trying to sabotage this in its familiar way: trying to perpetuate the process of "looking" to keep itself in business. It keeps insisting that *I haven't really seen this,* or *There is only mental understanding of this, not experiential.* But is this just thought up to its old tricks? Not sure. Certainly, there is a subtle sense of transparency around "Rowland," but there are still longer periods of contraction. Perhaps this is because of expectations here and an assumption that suffering will just drop away, or that there will be some grand change? This itself creates tension, I can see. So, there is both a feeling of being close to the Gate, and still being far away! And arising with this today is frustration, irritation with myself (*Why can't I get this clearly and quickly like other people?*), anxiety, guilt that I am taking up your time. But this is just what is happening, I guess. At other points this week there has been much more lightness. I think perhaps I need to keep digging and looking.

When "I" comes up hypnotically, have a good look, see if it can be found.

The "Rowland" I-thoughts need to be seen as an illusion, so that they don't keep snagging me when they come up. Perhaps I need to look a bit more closely at what a thought actually is. I have also decided to see a psychiatric nurse, and have made an appointment. I have had ongoing mental health issues for more than twenty years and seen various counselors, but I think now it needs to be addressed. Some of the mood swings I experience may simply be to do with a chemical imbalance in the brain, I suspect. Looking at the symptoms that seem to come up, it is a combination of bipolar and OCD, though I know these are just labels. However, there is less of a story attached to all of this now, less of a "me and my crazy emotions" story, and the various feelings that are triggered by it. It's not "me." But it's a bit like having a broken leg, it just seems sensible to see a doctor! Interestingly, mental illness (a terrible phrase) itself is quite a powerful pointer: if looked at clearly, it shows that nobody at all is at the helm. This is just stuff happening! Thank you so much for all your patience and kindness, Ilona, and for sticking by me with all these ups and downs. It does feel like things are starting to fall away, however much the mind might try to resist.

Much love, R.

Ilona: Hi Rowland. Yes, you have noticed it right, thoughts trigger contractions and the more they are resisted the harder it gets. Don't worry about how long it takes, it takes as long as needed. And it cannot be any other way for you. Trust that all that shows up is right.

I think perhaps I need to keep digging and looking.

When "I" comes up hypnotically, have a good look, see if it can be found.

The "Rowland" I-thoughts need to be seen as an illusion, so that they don't keep snagging me when they come up. Perhaps I need to look a bit more closely at what a thought actually is.

Very good point.

What is a thought?

Where does it come from?

Where does it go?

Can thoughts be controlled?

Is "I" a different thought? Is it more than a thought?

How about the thought "me"? Where does it point to?

If you take your finger and point now to this "me," where is the finger pointing to?

This is just stuff happening!

Yes! It's just stuff happening! Judging it as wrong or labeling it "illness"—does that make it so?

Big swings may be intense, but that, too, is just happening.

I cannot advise you about seeing a nurse or not, you know best what is right for you, just trust what feels like a big *yes*. Seeing through illusion does not change the character, nor what is happening, it just gives space for what shows up to play out without resistance.

You may also investigate *if* there is a mind.

What does the word "mind" point to?

Is there an invisible container of thoughts, memories, and hopes?

Or is it always just one thought after another, one thought at a time?

Thought says it is the mind thinking, but is there such a faculty as the mind doing thinking?

What do you see when you look here?

Much love.

Rowland: Thank you so much for your reply, dear Ilona! Sorry, I have taken a couple of days, but work has been especially busy, and I wanted to reflect clearly on the questions. Thank you too for your suggestion that I go with intuition in terms of seeing a doctor or nurse; it feels right at the moment.

There has been more lightness over the past couple of days, and less of a feeling of mood swings being "personal." "Rowland" has felt lighter, less serious. Just keep checking in with what is real and present: sensations, perceptions, thoughts, feelings, awareness of these. Just stuff coming up presently. Now and now and now, what is actually here. A thought is an object in awareness, it comes and goes like the sound of my fingers on the keyboard right now. It stops and starts. The thought *I like oranges* arises, and then drops away. After/before each thought is emptiness, silence. Awareness is not more aware of a thought than it is of the voices that can be heard outside right now. So a thought could be seen like a kind of sensation. If a thought is no closer than a sound, what makes it "mine"? This is conditioned thinking. It just feels like it's mine, feels like it refers to "me," or describes "me," or tells a story about a "me" with a past and a future, and with "shoulds" and "should nots," with ongoing problems and worries. Is any of this real? It just feels like it is inside something called "my head," but going on present evidence, is this true? There are sensations of a head, and thoughts presently arising, but there is no evidence that these are occurring inside those sensations. When a thought is looked at head-on, it can't be "what I am," as it is the object of noticing, like the sensations of this keyboard. It is just coming up neutrally in *what is*.

Where is the "I" to which thought refers? It exists nowhere except in thought.

If I were to point to "me," I would probably point towards head sensations. But does the I-thought necessarily have anything to do with these?

You may also investigate if there is a mind.

What do you see when you look here?

Where is the mind?

"Mind" is just another thought. It points to nothing. Going on present evidence, there is no container of thoughts. Just one thought at a time. It just struck me that thoughts only really refer to themselves, only to other thoughts. They only *seem* to refer to a reality. But they don't, as reality just *is*. Thoughts just *are*. Their meaning is only assumed. If the question "Where is the thinker?" is asked, there isn't one to be found. Just thoughts coming and going. Thank you again!

Much love, R.

Ilona: Hi Rowland. Oh yes, you're seeing it. Thoughts and sensory experiences don't touch each other. Thoughts are only referring to other thoughts. It's all thoughts about other thoughts. And this is also part of experience, part of what is happening.

How does it feel to see this?

What do you see now when you look at the character Rowland?

Is Rowland telling the story?

Is he driving what is happening?

Is there an actor that plays Rowland?

Is he the experiencer?

Show me what you see.

Big smile and hug.

Rowland: Thank you, dear Ilona! I hope this e-mail finds you well. I wrote quite a bit in my journal yesterday in response to your e-mail. I hope it makes sense, as I wrote fast!

How does it feel to see this?

It feels freeing to see this! There is less heaviness if the thought "I" is attached to sensations—it is just one more thing being noticed in awareness, one more sensation. Looking again now.

To which sensations does the I-thought refer?

Thought says "my body" because only "I can feel them," but where is this "I"? Where is the evidence? Right now, the sounds of the car outside, the birds chirping, the cat crunching his biscuits, his claws now clicking across the floor; these sounds are just as close as body sensations. There isn't really any "close," because there isn't really any "far away."

And with eyes closed; is there a distinction between body sensations and chair?

Despite the insistence of thought, it is impossible to say where "body" sensations end and "chair" sensations begin. It is all one flow. There is at the moment a lightness to seeing this, a subtle expansiveness and everything appearing equally here, in awareness. Listening to the birds right now; these sounds are inside awareness, the thoughts "I" or "Rowland" are inside awareness, the colors of my cat are inside awareness, but none of this is what I am. And is there an inside? It is all just stuff happening, coming and going, with a changelessly aware backdrop. (Is there even a backdrop?) Awareness is not an identity or person, it is just an ongoing, utterly pristine, noticing. More of a verb? Not a solid, or even ethereal, thing. But it is always here. Still flip-flopping with this, but seeing, too.

Where is the "I" that is flip-flopping?

Can't be found. Just sensations, feelings, coming and going, some thought labels "pleasant," some "unpleasant."

Where is this "I"?

My wife has just come downstairs and words (which can't be seen!) are coming out of something called a "mouth," these words are just happening. *Where is the "I" who is speaking?* So much love every-where! Only thought seems to prevent this from being seen.

What do you see now when you look at the character Rowland?

Is Rowland telling the story?

Is he driving what is happening?

Is there an actor that plays Rowland?

Is he the experiencer?

Show me what you see.

Rowland is an interesting character in the play of life! Loving, complicated, funny, warm, distant, shy, insecure, anxious, expansive, manic, withdrawn, compassionate, selfish, too sensitive, insensitive, addictive, troubled, frustrated…a bit of a colorful, rich mess! Suffering kicks in with the assumption that this is who I am, and that there is an "I" who can make things better, or improve, or be more spiritual, or could have been or done better. Suffering also kicks in with too much investment in any of these labels (Where is "withdrawn" or "too sensitive" in reality?). But there is nothing here other than sensations (even thoughts, feelings, perceptions could be seen as just things being sensed). Just what is coming up. And coming up. And coming up. What are the implications of this? It seems important to see these in reality. Might look into this a bit more. What exactly is this freedom? So "Rowland" does feel lighter at times—definitely. I feel like I am staring at the Gate, but then thought tells me I am not, that this is just intellectual! That I am just saying the right things, but it's just thought up to its old tricks! Although the "I" cannot be found, thought still seems to be potent and hypnotic at times.

Big smile and hug back to you! Thank you deeply for your amazing compassion and patience.

Ilona: Hi Rowland. I enjoyed reading that. Nice observations.

You say thoughts say that it's just intellectual. Do you believe this thought?

Take a look, is there a Gate to cross?

See what comes up when you ask the question "Is there an I?," rather than "*Where* is this I?"

Much love.

Rowland: Thank you, Ilona! When I ask the question "Is there an I?," the thought comes up, *No, there isn't, but it still feels at times like there is one.*

It is definitely being seen through more and more. What seems to happen at the moment is flip-flopping between a sense of lightness and ease and then something triggers conditioning, and the "I" solidifies again (or seems to). Fear and guilt often seem particularly to trigger the I-sense (the two emotions that have perhaps caused me the most difficulty since childhood).

For example, yesterday I happened across some writings on karma and the "unimaginable pains" of the lower realms in Mahayana Buddhism. (I think other forms of Buddhism speak of lower or hell realms as well, don't they?) This generated self-centered fear, even panic; and the "I" popped up immediately and a terror of experiencing this "myself" (What might "my" karmic debt be?), and also of this happening to others. Obsessive personal thoughts began churning and ruminating on past deeds, on karma. I could almost feel the "I" feeding on this! Real contraction. And then the thoughts, *What if this is correct? What if there are terrifying hell realms? How can I know for sure?* This began just digging away at me. It's a bit like spiritual hypochondria!

But I'm sitting with the fear, and the guilt, and the uncomfortable emotions, and the feeling of contraction. I'm having a good look at them. Who is feeling this fear? This guilt? Who is suffering? These emotions cover up the simple contentment of the present moment. They are thought's attempts to keep the story going. It doesn't want to be seen through! But are the emotions actually present? No, just labels imposed on raw sensation.

There is a bit of relief as I type this, as I look at what I've written. I think I need to keep away from spiritual websites and forums and stick to present-moment, direct experience. There is so much stuff out there, so many concepts, theories, perspectives, beliefs. What is true *now?*

Much love.

Ilona: Okay, consider this: there is no "who." It's a construct of language, useful in communicating and storytelling. But, there is no "who" outside of language. If language was made just of verbs alone, such questions as "who" or "what" would not arise.

"Who" points to a separate entity, subject, but *is* there a subject that experiences or is experiencing happening?

What is true in your experience?

Is there a "who"?

Is there a "what"?

Is there a gap between perceiver and perceived?

Is there someone or something that feels guilt?

Are sensations of contraction happening to some perceiver?

Is seeing happening to a seer?

Sending love.

Rowland: Thank you, dear Ilona! The Gateless Gate seems nearer and nearer.

Okay, consider this: there is no "who." It's a construct of language, useful in communicating and storytelling. But, there is no "who" outside of language.

This is becoming clearer and clearer, Ilona. Without language, where are any problems?

If language was made just of verbs alone, such questions as "who" or "what" would not arise.

There would be such freedom too. It is I/you/they that creates problems, responsibilities, debts, pressures, shoulds, should nots, conflicts, difficulties, worries. Without these, there would just be the spontaneous arising of sensations. No judging. No ongoing, painful stories. Without the I-thought, where is the person with a problematic past/present/future? With obligations? This is real freedom and just needs to be totally felt and seen, I think. Really felt and seen. At the moment it feels like there are glimpses of the light.

"Who" points to a separate entity, subject, but is there a subject that experiences or is experiencing happening?

Looking now, there definitely isn't one. It is just not there. Throughout the day I pause to have a look—particularly when difficult thoughts or memories are coming up—and there are only the thoughts, feelings, sensations. I can't find a center to them. Who is there to believe that thoughts are true?

What is true in your experience?

Is there a "who"?

Is there a "what"?

Is there a gap between perceiver and perceived?

Is there someone or something that feels guilt?

Are sensations of contraction happening to some perceiver?

Is seeing happening to a seer?

There is no "who," and not even a "what." It is difficult to say anything beyond "there is noticing of sensations." There is noticing of what is coming up right now. A gap between perceiver and perceived cannot be found either.

What would hearing be without the object of hearing? Where does "hearing" end and the sound of voices begin? Where does the "seeing" of this computer end and the computer itself begin? Nothing can be separated out.

No feeler of guilt or fear can be found—just thoughts, anxious sensations, presently arising. But none at the moment. My sense is that

I am seeing this pretty clearly now, but that conditioning/patterns just need to be thoroughly seen through, as they come up with such force. Guilt and fear have been such strong emotions since childhood. Just need to keep questioning assumptions and thoughts.

Love and light!

Ilona: Yes, right here, spot on. Let this just settle in. Keep noticing and looking. Focus on what is already obvious; instead of looking for what is not there, look at *what is*.

Is there anything, anyone that owns conditioning?

Sending love.

Rowland: Thank you, Ilona. Yes, I think I need to settle in with this, to keep looking, to get really clear. What I am finding at the moment is that there is no "I" to be found and there are periods of lightness as this is seen, and then thought seems to come in with such hypnotic and compelling force, it almost feels overpowering! It feels so hard not to listen to the self-critical thought-voice, particularly when it starts drawing on painful stories and memories. As you suggest, focus on what is real: sensations, colors, sounds—all arising right now in awareness. Everything else is story. This is so clear as I write this. Thank you for sticking with me, Ilona. I am so deeply grateful to you.

Love, R.

Ilona: Great stuff.

Now look, is there anyone who gets lost in a story or is it just more story arising?

Examine the voice in the head. Is there a listener to which it is talking?

Does the voice know what is true or does it thinks that it knows?

Much love.

Rowland: Thanks, Ilona! Hope you are enjoying the sunny weather! I sat quietly yesterday and spent some time inquiring into thought.

Yes, the idea that there is anyone who gets lost in a story is just more story! There are stories that arise; thoughts, memories, images, but (if I am really honest) nobody there to take ownership of them. They are not "my" stories, "my" memories. Thoughts appear, like sensations and perceptions appear, in impersonal awareness.

So there is no need to "do" anything with thoughts any more than there is a need to "do" anything with the sound of a blackbird on a roof. The key for me at the moment is not to be afraid of, or frustrated by, thought as if it is waiting in the wings, and might spring out at any moment to hypnotize me and draw me in! I think I still attribute too much power to thought. I still get irritated sometimes that thought is so busy that I rarely achieve a state of "spiritual stillness." But, of course, the more I want a quiet mind, the more it will elude me. I spent much of yesterday feeling light and unencumbered with "me": it was so clear that life, no matter what is arising, does not know worries and problems. This is just the natural way of being! Tomorrow I have my appointment with the doctor to discuss "my" (!) OCD/bipolar traits, but again, this is not an identity. Just stuff that is arising and needs to be looked at! Take care. Lots of love and gratitude.

Ilona: Nice! I can see that the veil is lifting.

Look at thought itself. How does it happen that it gets believed?

What is a belief?

How does it work?

Is any belief true?

If so, what makes it true?

Sending love.

Rowland: Attention and energy go to the thought, such that it is believed and becomes "true." But any thought is a belief, and therefore no thought is really "true." Even memory thoughts, which seem to be "more" than thoughts, which seem to solidify the separate self (*I did such and such...*, *I used to do x, y, z...*, and so forth), even these are beliefs, as they rely on the reality of the "I."

It hit me a couple of days ago that any thought which contains a statement about "I" is ultimately a fiction. It's like the implications of this freedom are beginning to trickle through with the mind not wanting them to be seen, wanting to keep the prison running, however subtly. Even the thought *I bought a bottle of water yesterday* relies on three assumptions: that there is an "I"; that there is a separate, self-contained, independent object (a bottle of water); and that there is, in reality, something concrete ("back there") called "yesterday." But these are all just assumptions.

All there is, is what is happening right now. Thoughts, sensations, feelings, arising in unchanging awareness. Those thoughts/feelings/sensations aren't necessarily related to one another as an "entity" either; this is another assumption. What does the thought *I am typing* necessarily have to do with the physical sensations of typing, beyond the fact that this is all experienced in/by awareness? This is so freeing! If no thought is believed, there is only natural freedom. I need to keep coming back to this, seeing this, even though there is no "I" to do this (!). That is just more of the prison.

I found myself yesterday getting into the trap of *Should I or should I not practice?* and reading what different teachers say—strong arguments both ways. And then thoughts would arise like: *It's okay to practice if I am not expecting anything from it. But how do I know if I am expecting something or not?* Again, all this suffering/confusion/frustration is thought. All of it.

I will continue to sit quietly in the evening, inquiring and looking until I don't. I just enjoy it.

Take care, Ilona! It has been lovely seeing the sunshine over the last few days, the countryside bristling with butterflies and honeybees!

Love and light.

Ilona: Oh, I love this warm sunshine! And I have the sea five minutes down the road. Really nice to feel warm. Yes, yes, yes, this is very clear. Practice or no practice? How about both. Practice happens when it happens and then it's not practice, but arising in awareness. Just meditate. Expectations, too, are only thoughts about thoughts. Yes, let this settle and enjoy the ride. Can you say you are ready for the final questions?

Much love.

Rowland: Thanks so much, Ilona, glad you are enjoying the sun! Could I possibly stay with this for a week or two, and get back to you? I feel like I still need to settle in with the seeing, to really "get" the implications of it. We are off to Norfolk tomorrow until Monday. Have a brilliant weekend!

Much love.

Ilona: Sure, Rowland, get back to me when it's the right time. For now, have a wonderful time!

Sending lots of love!

Rowland: Hi Ilona. How are you? Hope you have had a great two weeks, and have been enjoying the sunshine by the sea! We are off tomorrow to the Whitby Coast for a long weekend.

The sea is such a good reminder, always present and yet never the same from moment to moment! A mass of beautiful, shifting, changing sensations, ceaselessly tumbling into and out of new forms and yet always "the sea"!

Over the last couple of weeks, I have certainly felt more freedom and spaciousness, and thoughts have a bit less "sting." Much more of a sense of just being here with what arises. Rowland is far less solid than he used to be! Thoughts/situations do come up and seem to "snag" me, but with a bit of looking, I can't find anyone who is being "snagged" or "caught."

It is like I am kind of growing into freedom, like a child taking baby steps, two steps forward, two back, three forward, two back.

On Tuesday I saw a consultant who told me (as an initial assessment) that he thought I had a combination of OCD and borderline personality disorder (BPD), which I have always suspected. It's interesting, though: these are clearly just labels now, nothing to be owned or taken personally. It is just what is happening. No need to worry about what will happen in the future either, as this will also just be what is happening! Sensations arising in a peaceful sea of awareness. When the consultant told me what he thought was going on with me, there was just a calm (even slightly amused) watching of the situation. Nothing really to get caught up in. Thank you so much for everything, Ilona, you guys at Liberation Unleashed do a truly amazing job holding people's hands and guiding them so generously and wisely and patiently as they begin to see what is actually real and happening. To be honest, there is no way to express gratitude that is adequate, but *thank you*!

Much love, Rowland.

Ilona: Hi Rowland, So delightful to read your e-mail. I can see that relaxation is taking place, and that puts a huge smile on my face. Okay, so you say that Rowland is less solid. Good. Now let's look deeper.

Where is the solid part?

What is here that indicates that Rowland is here?

What is Rowland made of?

How do you know?

Where is Rowland now?

Can you get rid of him?

Do you need to get rid of him?

What comes up here?

Much love.

Rowland: Thanks so much for your reply, Ilona!

The only "solidity" Rowland seems to have is, from time to time, in thought/memory. Otherwise he can't be found. And sometimes thought seems to add itself to uncomfortable sensations/feelings, which creates more of a feeling of a solid "me."

Over the past couple of days, my mood has gone up and down in quite intense ways—irritable, anxious, talkative, and so forth—and sometimes these mood swings are accompanied by automatic resistant or judgemental thinking (*This shouldn't be happening after all this inquiry!*; *This is OCD/BPD stuff*; *I'm crazy!*; *I'm so far from enlightened!*; *There shouldn't be so much thinking!*; and so forth). But is any of it happening to a "me"?

However uncomfortable sensations might be, they aren't happening to a "me." There is no "me" or "Rowland" to be found, except (seemingly) in the next thought. There is no "me" making anything happen, or being responsible for what is happening, or taking charge of it, or directing it. There is no "me" to make it go away. If the question "Who is thinking?" is asked, no thinker/doer can be found, just thoughts popping up spontaneously, referring to other thoughts.

Thank you!

Love, R.

Ilona: Thank you for answers and yay! Yes, the thoughts can come up, but they don't need to stick. Just like weather changes, so do the mood and sensations; when you see that it's just happening, there is no more suffering over "unpleasant" events. They come and go. No need to hold on to pleasant events either, they come and go too. There is freedom in experiencing this impermanence. So…

Can you say that, yes, it's clear that "I" is not an entity in charge?

If not, what else can we look at?

Much love.

Rowland: Hi Ilona. Thank you so much, as ever, for your patience! I would say it is about 99.9 percent clear now that no entity is in charge, that sensations, and events, come and go.

Even in the midst of "difficult" moods it is clear that "I" am not causing them, or causing "difficult" events. Everything just flows in and out, like the tide, in the sea of awareness. Sometimes thoughts/ stories seem to hook (which I guess is inevitable after decades of conditioning), but with a quick question—like "Where is this 'I'?"— the thoughts can be seen for what they are: impersonal, not refer- ring or belonging to anyone, not coming out of (or going) anywhere.

The one thing I would like to look at just a little more is time/ memory, which can still hypnotize "me" most strongly; it is the one thing that still does (although not nearly as much as it used to). Painful memories resurface and powerfully seem to construct the "I" to which they refer. What is the best way to really see through these? I feel like I am so nearly there, so nearly ready for the final questions!

Take care.

Love and light.

Ilona: Great! Almost there. Okay, look at memories this way: they arise, so they can be looked at, feelings felt and released. The repressed memories are charged with unwanted feelings. The more these feelings get released, the less memories will surface. In a while they won't trigger feelings anymore. So, instead of resisting these memories, try the opposite. Invite them to come up.

A good way to work with this is by writing. Draw a long line. On the left put a dot, your birthday. On the right put a dot, this is now. Then mark the time line and search for painful memories, mark them all on the line. Write down each one of them. Welcome each one of them into this presence and see if there is a theme running through. Examine and answer these questions:

Was there a separate self in these situations?

Could anything have been different at any of those times?

How does a memory arise?

How is a memory experienced?

Is there anything here, right now, that owns these memories?

At the end, once these questions are answered, go to each memory and give a hug to young Rowland. Tell him that you love him very much and always will. Write me a report on what happens.

Much love your way.

Rowland: Hi Ilona. Thank you so much. I think I am basically there!

Below are my answers to the questions, which I wrote over the weekend (and I added one more question: "Is there a past back there in which events happened?"). Hope they make sense.

It is an interesting time: just as I am about to see a psychologist after the diagnosis of BPD, the very self seems to be evaporating! But the conditioning does still need seeing through and working out, as it will continue to come up and cause suffering. Painful behaviors/feelings/compulsions here, but nobody around to take delivery of them!

The first thing I noticed was that, stretching right back to child-hood, lots of memories have to do with shame, guilt, anger, or resentment. Almost as far back as I can remember. Saying how much I love the "young Rowland" after the inquiry brought up tears, and a sense of natural compassion (it became clear how little "self-compassion" has really been experienced here in this lifetime).

Was there a separate self in these situations?

No separate self in any situation, nobody controlling, or guiding, or who could have acted any differently. No real "situations," just a flow of passing, never-to-be-repeated sensations. Is there a separate self here now, writing this? No. Fingers on a keyboard, sound of the keys, cars outside, breathing, thoughts popping up from time to time, arguing against this, but where is the one thinking? Silence.

Could anything have been different at any of those times?

Nothing could have been different because nobody, anywhere, is in control. Where is any "person" in those situations? Therefore, where are such things as guilt/blame/debt/issues still needing attention and so forth? Who would be going back into the "past"? Experience is only, effortlessly, *now*.

How does a memory arise?

A memory arises, completely spontaneously, in the present moment. Nobody is remembering. There is no "rememberer."

How is a memory experienced?

A memory is always experienced *now*. But it is like a passing sensation, it is not personal. There is no evidence that it even refers back to anything other than another thought, so why get weighed down by something that doesn't have any solid, independent reality? Who is there to "be" weighed down? Do any present sensations have any past or future? None. They are always fresh, history-less. (For example, the sensations labeled "foot" are all presently occurring for the first time, not referring back to a story of "previous sensations of foot"!) *What is* has no historical baggage. It is lighter than light, in truth. This is how life lives itself, whether this is seen or not.

Is there anything here, right now, that owns these memories?

Nobody owns those memories. A thought cannot own another thought. No memory refers to anything actual/substantial—just another thought, threaded through the I-thought. Presently arising sensations do not own or hold on to anything at all. Life itself is *now*. Being is *now*. If the memory/thought arises, such as *I did such and such* or *They did such and such*, to whom does this thought refer? There is no "I"/"they" to "do" or to "not do" anything, to claim or blame. Physical sensations/sense perceptions do not make an "I." Nor is there a "they" or "he"/"she"/"you" out there responsible for anything. Sensations/perceptions do not act, they just arise spontaneously in awareness.

Is there a past back there in which events happened?

Where is "the past"? Thought paints a very convincing picture, but the past only arises *now* in thought. It doesn't exist "somewhere else" as if it were waiting for thought to "reveal" it. It is re-created moment by moment, and each thought is totally new. There is no past to be "gone back into," and nobody to "need" to do this, either. Everything is spontaneously, innocently, coming and going, coming and going, never to be repeated or "carried around" or taken personally. Hope this makes sense! Thank you again for everything, Ilona, I think I am ready for the final questions! Much love.

Ilona: Wonderful to hear! Love your answers. Looks like the past has been seen through. And here are some new questions for you. Please answer in full, when ready.

Much love.

Some time later…

Rowland: Hi Ilona. Below are my answers! Thank you so, so very much, and please let me know if I can do anything to help in the future. It is an interesting time: with BPD, "difficult" feelings/thoughts/behaviors inevitably will come up; and there will be days, I am sure, where the separate self will seem to reassert itself (although, who knows). But right now, Rowland can't be found. I would love to write something, at some point, on mental illness and seeing through the separate self. Perhaps it would help others who find themselves in a similar situation.

Much love, and keep in touch!

1. Is there a separate entity "self," "me," "I" at all, anywhere, in any way, shape, or form? Was there ever?

No, there is no separate entity, no "I," "me," "you" anywhere. There can't be, as separation cannot be found. Just the free play of sensations and perceptions in awareness: nobody is controlling, directing, or shaping it. Even thought that insists "it" is doing something, or acting independently in some way, is spontaneously arising. Thought can be very hypnotic, seductive, after a lifetime of conditioning, but when looked at, all of its claims are empty. Even the thoughts *Thought is very seductive* or *There is a lifetime of conditioning* are empty, not ultimately true. Not only is there no separate entity, there never has been. And even more than this, strictly speaking, there never has been *anything*. Sensations and perceptions arise spontaneously, moment by moment, and for the first time. Each sensation, including the sensation of thought, is totally free of historical baggage. The "past" (like the "future") is just another spontaneously arising thought. It has no substance. And if there is no continuity in time, where is the separate self?

2. Explain in detail what the illusion of separate self is, when it starts, and how it works from your own experience. Describe it fully as you see it now.

The separate self-illusion begins in early childhood (perhaps around the age of two): A baby is born without any story, sense of individuation, sense of "problems," and so on. It doesn't even conceive of itself as a "baby"! What we refer to as "baby" is (from the baby's perspective) just a dance of sensations without end, only ever in the moment, beautiful and borderless and immediate. The separate self is the illusion that one is an individual human—apart from others, apart from the world, but with control, volition, past, and future. The body becomes a historical boundary, rather than just a present play of perception; thought becomes "my thought" and "thoughts about me" and begins to reference an imagined self-center. Life becomes heavy, burdensome, loses its lightness as responsibility kicks in, and gets heavier and heavier.

The separate self, as it (apparently) grows older, feels more and more distant from the world/others, more and more defective, and less and less able to live up to standards imposed from a perceived "outside," and also from an apparent "inside." In my experience, life becomes very difficult: pushing harder and harder against the tide becomes the norm. The "inner" narrative for some apparent individuals becomes more painful with each passing decade, with increased "history" and concern about "future."

What began as a spontaneous dance becomes more like the trudge of a prisoner in a chain gang, who has no idea when he/she may be released—or if he/she ever will be free.

Spirituality can then add to this difficult story: as we begin to read "spiritual" books, we might think we are returning to the dance, but often we are adding more rules, obligations, and "future" concern. We miss the fact that the dance has been happening all along, we have just missed it! The chain gang is a dream; the chains are not real. The dance is. The dance is happening.

3. How does it feel to see this? What is the difference from before you started this dialogue? Please report from the past few days.

Although there are still challenges here—I have been diagnosed with a psychological disorder and am undergoing treatment—life is lighter, easier. There isn't nearly as much guilty rumination, or anxious forward thinking. Life is taking care of itself; and there is nobody at the wheel. What is happening is happening. We may label bits of it "painful," but these are just words. Everything is just arising spontaneously, so why worry, why regret? Why look backward, why look forward? Life itself never does. From moment to moment, moods might shift, thought might come back in and (seemingly) try to take center stage again, asserting the unhappy "me," but if this is looked for, it cannot be found. And this is all just happening in the only way it can. All of it.

4. What was the last bit that pushed you over? What made you look?

For me, one of the most powerful recognitions was seeing the insubstantiality of the past, and of time generally. Memory, perhaps more than anything, was sustaining the unhappy narrative of "me." Seeing that there is only ever *now*, but actually seeing it and investigating it rather than just reading about it, was important. Time is created moment by moment, and fades moment by moment.

5. Do you decide, intend, choose, control events in life? Do you make anything happen? Give examples from your experience.

No, there is nobody to decide, choose, or control events in life. We cannot even say life chooses/controls/decides, as that would be to personify life, and give it an agenda. There is nobody here to decide and I don't think I can even say that "decisions happen," as the word "decision" still sounds too definitive, too much like there is a separate agent in the mix. Rather, events happen—whether those events are thoughts, feelings, perceptions. A so-called decision is just another event, coming and going in the flow of awareness. I am not making these words happen now, they are appearing as I type on the screen; but they are just happening, as are the thoughts that are running alongside them, as is the sound of cars, as is the sound of my cat's claws on the dining-room floor. Where is the "me" in any of this? Why should thoughts be about "me" when the sounds of the cars clearly are not? Why the division? It is the same with a psychological disorder: I have not made this happen, nor has anyone else. It is a happening, too; and even to call it a "psychological disorder" presumes a past history which, actually, when looked for, cannot be found. It is just another series of constantly shifting, changing events, and there is no way of knowing what will happen. Who would want to know, anyway? What a beautiful mystery!

6. Anything to add?

I would mainly like to add my deep, deep gratitude to Ilona and everyone at the Liberation Unleashed website: what you guys do is generous and important beyond words, and a true outpouring of love. *Thank you!*

Ilona: Wow. That is as clear as it gets. Thank you for wonderful answers and the whole process. I can already see how this has potential to help people that go through the same story as you. I would love to share this with readers of my blog, with your permission, of course. I don't need to use your real name, let me know what you prefer. I am really, really happy for you. And I know you will be just fine. Your mind is not broken, it's perfect and you express clearly and simply; I can see, you would be a good guide. Sending you a big hug and lots of love.

Rowland: Hey Ilona. Thanks for your lovely e-mail! No worries at all with posting our dialogue on your blog. I am sure it will be okay to use "Rowland." It would be really nice to help others, too. Take care, and have a great evening! Much love.

A few months later, I asked Rowland to share how he was doing. Here is what he wrote:

Since finishing the Liberation Unleashed investigation with dear Ilona, a number of things have become much clearer. The presence of a substantial, separate entity called "Rowland" has become very difficult indeed to find: it is evident, when looked at, that thoughts like *I* and *me* float through experiencing, like leaves do in the wind on a delicious autumn day. Where and what is this "me"? There is a looking back and…silence. Just this. And where is the one who decides, controls, chooses, wills? He, too, is a phantom, a thought's thought, perhaps.

But equally, challenges have arisen (and do arise). Even when it is clear that there is no separate "I" to speak of, thought can still surge up with hypnotic force, asking to be looked at, seen through. Some days this happens often—in times of stress, for example—and on other days, less so. But who is there to want or will this otherwise? Only "I" can have a problem with the arising of an "I."

It has also been interesting in that, simultaneous with the initial seeing-through of Rowland, I have been diagnosed with a mood disorder and am about to begin a course of psychological treatment as an outpatient. Old patterns and conditioning have flared painfully at times, addictions, mood swings, racing thoughts, manic overactivity giving way at points to sloth and frightening depression. But with all this said, there is certainly much greater acceptance than before: less of a need to turn it into a personal melodrama of cause and effect. It's happening, like storms sometimes happen, and sunny days too. There is nobody, really, choosing it or not choosing it.

And—weirdly—there is something kind of beautiful in the unpredictable, whirligig patterning of labels and thoughts; there is no reaching for judgements. In a way, (what is called) mental illness is a great teacher: it is a reminder that we are not separate from life; that there is nobody home to dictate the course of events; that the wind will blow as it blows. Maybe we'll like it, maybe not! But who's—and what's—not to like? Hmm.

There has also been a definite heart opening: a sense of overwhelming love at times for (seemingly) others, whether animals, humans, or even (so-called) inanimate objects. Everything shines if we look. It does. Even, or especially, when it rains. It feels like neither the words "personal" nor "impersonal" are quite right. Nor even the word "love." It seems like it is more about just seeing what is really there, what is really happening, in every blessed moment.

I continue to meditate, sit, rest, investigate, but with more spontaneity and curiosity now, and less of a sense of *Damn! I just need to get there!* It is wonderful just to look and see what is right here, right now. To see what is shining always, imperturbably, in and through the whole show.

Thank you, Ilona! The work you guys do is so much appreciated. I hope to be able to return the gift soon.

Deep Looking

Are you at peace right now? If so, nice. If not, then let me introduce you to a very simple way to peace. I call this technique "Deep Looking." It is a blend of different kinds of releasing techniques and is loosely based on the Sedona method (http://www.sedona.com /Home.asp) and Pamela Wilson's way of talking to the heart and mind (http://pamelasatsang.com), which I witnessed at a couple of satsangs.

First, before we start Deep Looking, I'd like you to notice again how the mind labels everything. Where focus goes, thinking follows. If you look to the left and notice what is there right now, watch what happens with thoughts—they label and describe the scene. They name shapes, colors, objects. Those labels may trigger a memory, so a little story may come up. Words flow when focus touches what is there. (When you see something clearly, you can describe what is seen.)

> **Try This for Yourself** Where focus goes, thinking follows.
> Bring focus to how you feel right now.
> Describe it in a few words for yourself.
> Notice words that label feelings arise when attention goes to the feelings.
> Just play a little and observe how it all works.

It's one thing to see that a separate self is an illusion, but it's quite another to end the resisting of *what is*. It's as if there are layers to awakening, one more subtle than the layer just peeled away. Seeing that no one is here doing, thinking, living a life of a separate

entity does not automatically end all resistance. It's not a one-hit-
and-that's-it, resistance-no-longer-arises kind of deal. All those little
thoughts, beliefs, shoulds, emotional wounds, fears, habits, stories—
the whole personality of the character—did not form in a day, so
they do not usually collapse in a day either.

If you look back at your life, there is a story. Some stories are
sticky, some are vague, some trigger deep emotional pain—the pain
that paralyzes and keeps one stuck in the same patterns. If you could
release all this sad stuff, what would be left is pure joy of being and
peace.

When resistance ends, surrendering happens; both are actually
the same movement, labeled from opposite viewpoints. Every little
resistance released is surrendering in action. It's a letting go, a falling
off of old "parts of you," of stuff that no longer serves and is no
longer needed.

Yes, So Be It

So be it. Let all the stuff that no longer serves get deconstructed,
uncreated, released, dissolved, melted away, and gone. Who needs
those fear-laden patterns, right? So be it. Whatever happens in the
process of releasing is okay.

If fear comes up, it's only here to show you that you are entering
unexplored areas; it signals that something feels protected and does
not want to be seen. Let that be okay as well.

Welcoming

It may feel silly or even funny, but welcoming everything that comes
up is key. It's very important. Kindness, openness, gentleness, compassion, softness, honesty, and love are door openers. When pushing
stops, allowing begins. Welcoming is not a weakness but a most
powerful, underrated tool in the mission of clearing the feeling of
being stuck. But what good is the tool if it's not being used?

"Thank You" Is the Magic Phrase

Thanking whatever shows up turns the feeling about it around. Resistance turns into acceptance. "Thanking" is the alchemy of feeling. It's the main principle of Deep Looking. Welcoming, thanking, and giving space for the feeling to enfold you and be here opens the door for it to pass. You can bow in honor and hug and kiss the feeling, the mind, and the heart. The response to thanking is one of opening, of feeling appreciation, compassion, and love.

Try thanking whatever is present right now, before reading further.

Try This for Yourself   Thank the heart and the mind, literally, for being beautiful and gorgeous.

Give them both a warm hug and a smile.

Tell them that you love them so much. Bow in honor and in appreciation.

Say, "Thank you. I love you."

That's it. If there is resistance, it's fine. Thank the resistance for doing such a great job of protecting whatever needs to be protected. Give a hug to resistance, even if it sounds a bit crazy. Accepting resistance brings you a step closer to releasing it. After all, resistance is a friend.

Listening Deeply to What the Mind and the Heart Have to Say

The Deep Looking process is a conversation with whatever structure comes up to talk. When you turn focus inward, notice that there is a voice talking. This voice labels everything. Using this function of the mind, we can have a chat with the mind, heart, and body to see what they want.

When we listen to how the mind and heart respond, we can take the next step, which is to ask another question that rises up from the previous answer. Whatever shows up in the answer is showing the way to go deeper. Craft another question from the previous answer.

Talking to the mind may sound weird, but it's no more weird than the conversations we sometimes have in our head with partners or parents, rehearsing what we might say or running old tapes.

Talking to the mind is role play, a game; don't take it too seriously. Doing so does not mean that there are entities called Mind or Heart that live inside the entity called Body. It only means that if you ask a question of the structure directly, you get a direct answer. Simple.

Try This for Yourself   Ask the mind if it's at peace. Literally.

"Mind, are you at peace?"

It's either yes or no.

Wait for the answer.

… … … …

If yes, then thank the mind for the answer and ask the heart the same question.

"Heart, are you at peace?"

Wait for the answer, and if it comes as yes, then thank the heart too and enjoy the rest of the day.

If no comes up, ask the mind/heart what it wants the most.

You may write the answers down, as this helps to keep focus.

… … … …

After each answer give thanks and honor to the heart and the mind, or whatever you are talking to at that moment.

… … … …

Now ask the mind, what it wants the most. Wait for an answer, and listen closely. You may be surprised, so allow the answer to be heard, and *acknowledge* the heart's or mind's desire.

Then ask what is in the way of having this now.

When the answer comes, welcome it. Notice the feeling that accompanies it, and let that feeling be here for a minute.

And just allow it to be as it is. You can talk to that feeling as well and ask it what it wants. Play with it and see what comes up, and keep listening and noticing bodily sensations.

… … … …

You may check in with the mind and heart:

"Are you ready to relax?"

If you get a yes, ask the next question:

"Are you ready to relax now?"

If both answers are yes, then just close your eyes and feel.

Feel fully, without putting labels on what is felt.

Just let the raw sensations enfold you, play out, and pass. Take your time with this exercise, and when it feels that all has passed, bring in more sensations, and feel them out, and then bring in some more. And even more. Keep at the process—welcoming, bringing up, feeling out—as long as it feels right. You might imagine that there is an open door in the area of the feeling; see how the feeling is moving through that door. Alternatively, just feel. In the end the feeling may be exhaustion, tiredness. That's okay. This work requires a bit of concentration.

When feelings like fear or resistance come up, talk to them and ask what it is they are protecting. When you get an answer, ask the mind to *look* to see if it still needs to protect that, or if protection is no longer needed. If protection is no longer needed, you may ask if the feeling wants to leave. If it says yes, then feel it out as described above. If the answer is no, then ask what this feeling wants to tell you. Listen. Whatever the answer is, thank the feeling for the answer and focus on what comes up in the answer. This all may sound a bit complicated, but when you are there, in conversation, the questions and answers just play out by themselves.

The only thing to keep an eye on is focus. Stay focused.

Distraction (Again)

The tricky thing is, if you are coming close to some strongly protected area of the heart, mind, or body, which feels like strong resistance, the defense mechanism ignites. It shows up as a sudden boredom, laziness (not wanting to carry on), sleepiness, dismissal, or blankness. The mind jumps to defense mode and either builds a wall or creates a distraction, or both.

Distraction can come in many forms. You may suddenly feel that you have something else to do, or your focus goes to something completely unrelated, something that appears to be much more interesting. Distraction is a trick that the mind plays when something feels threatened. If you notice this happen, bring the focus back gently.

Tell the mind that it is safe and that you are here only to help it get what it wants the most.

Keep looking, keep welcoming, and focus on what else there is that wants to speak up.

Often scenes from childhood come up: a little kid, a child version of you, who may feel unloved, abandoned, and wants to be heard. If hurt is still there, there is something unresolved that needs attention, processing, and acceptance.

Hug that child and tell her how precious and beautiful she is and how very much you love her.

Have a heart-to-heart conversation and express openly how you feel about her as well as listen attentively to what she has to say to you. Stay with her till she feels lighter.

Protection

Everyone has protective mechanisms, both "outer" and "inner," for good and practical reasons. But when you look inside and ask "What is here that needs to be protected right now?," the answer that comes may be a surprise. You may see that the mind creates and protects images.

Images do not need to be protected, as there is nothing that can harm a mere image in any way. Think about it: What is the worst thing that can happen to an image? However, the protection mechanism may still start up.

Try This for Yourself   Simply ask yourself, "Is it true, does this still need to be protected?"

If the answer is yes, then find out what is really feeling threatened.

Keep looking deeper, and look behind the fear.

What is there?

When you see that there is nothing that needs to be protected, when you really see that, the structure of protection collapses. It becomes obvious that this protection is guarding only an idea, not something that is really present. Nothing can be harmed in any way, because it's nothing. Emptiness.

I've had many Deep Looking sessions with many people, and in only a few cases did big release not happen, and when it didn't happen, it only meant that more patience was needed to unlock the old, rusty locks. Many sessions ended with people feeling light and blissful or falling asleep; sometimes I fell asleep too, as it does take a lot of concentration to go all the way through the process till the end. But what I noticed is that when a client releases, release happens for both people participating in the session. It is quite interesting to be part of this process as deepening of peace happens for both people.

Anyway, theory is one thing, reading or listening to someone else's process is another, but diving right in and trying Deep Looking for yourself is something that has to be experienced. You can do it anywhere, anytime—in the middle of busy day or while meditating. Directness, immediacy, and intimacy are right here, in the asking of a direct question, from which authentic action can arise.

In the beginning, it may feel strange to talk to the heart and mind, especially if you see that "mind" and "heart" are just labels, empty ideas. But give it a try, explore this method and see for yourself. It may get you into deeper peace, and there is nothing at all to fear or to lose using this method. If it doesn't work for you, never mind.

If you find the method useful, share it with a friend, pass it on, try it with someone, and experiment. Find what works for you. Peace is already here, waiting to be noticed.

It's a mystery how Deep Looking works, but it surely does. The process allows you to go right to the root of stuck energy. It lets you examine the beliefs and feelings around an issue, and a release happens, a deep release that clears the space around the issue. Deep Looking fills the space where tightness and unease used to be with love and appreciation.

When the mind and heart are content and at peace, you can ask the mind if it knows that the heart is its home.

Ask the mind if it is already at home, and if the answer is no, ask the mind if it wants to go home, to join with the heart.

Make sure both sides, the mind and the heart, agree, and then just close your eyes for a few minutes and feel the heart. You can put a hand on the chest to make the sensation more vivid. Then just close your eyes for a bit and feel the heart.

Feel the energy moving and simply be with it.

Descriptions fail at this point; there is no need to name the feeling.

After this release, the opening continues. There may be more issues left to release, so the opening will unfold through the next few days. Release is an energetic shift, a change in how you relate to *what is*, how you feel most of the time—a new default frequency.

If you use the Deep Looking technique by yourself, it may take patience and time. Each time you use it, there is a little release. In a few days or weeks, there will be a noticeable difference. If you use this technique with a partner, somebody who helps you hold the focus, the release can be really big and sudden. The whole point of a having a partner is to have someone to keep you at it, all the way through.

When I first started using this technique, I did it by myself, but then I started practicing it with friends and people I had never met. It is amazing to see from the inside how the mind mechanisms work. The mind protects the heart. In this noble task it became confused, and suffering was created. Instead of looking for the root cause and releasing it, the mind created more and more security structures to protect the heart from suffering, and that only created more suffering. In the end, the heart may feel small, wounded, and helpless. All the heart wants is to love. It can love freely, but the mind keeps it "safe" from possible hurt. Sometimes it offers protection *just in case*, without examining if that protection works for the good or only creates more tension.

The heart is at peace when it's expanded, limitless, conditionless—when it loves what it loves and enjoys the feeling of it.

If you listen to what your mind and heart really want, if you start to communicate with those two, eventually the knot will loosen and the tightness will melt away. What is left is openness and acceptance. Peace with *what is*.

You can communicate with the body, too. You can ask yes and no questions and see what reactions appear—opening sensations, or expansion, are a yes; closing and tightness, or contraction, are a no. It's very simple. And Deep Looking works with physical symptoms, too. Behind physical symptoms there are often unconscious mechanisms of the mind.

Friederich

My conversation with Friederich took three months. It wasn't a joyful time, and the process was not quick, but the transformation that happened was beautiful. We talked about how story creates itself, then resistance came up, and our conversation became intense. Anger, hate, and desperation came up. We had a Deep Looking session, and he was able to relax. I was so happy for him.

[Note to the reader: English is not Friederich's first language, so we had to revise some of his words, while retaining the meaning and his unique voice.]

Friederich: Hi Ilona, I found your e-mail address in your book *Gateless Gatecrashers*.

Although it would seem that "I" have a "clear" understanding that there isn't really any "me," the sense of it is still rather strong! So, clearly, clear seeing hasn't happened—yet. But, hopefully, the time is ripe for it. So please, let me know if we can communicate through this medium, or if we would have to do it through your forum! Thanks for reading.

Ilona: Hi Friederich. Thank you for your message, it's great to hear from you. Yes, we can communicate through this medium, and it would be my pleasure to have a chat with you. Here are some questions for you to ponder:

Focus on the sense of "me." What is it? Where is it? Is it a sense of being/aliveness, or a sense of "me"? Does that sense disappear if it's labeled differently, let's say, "broccoli"?

Is the sense of being happening to you? Or as you? Is there "you" in the sense or only in thought? Without thought does the sense of being disappear?

Is sense of being personal? Is there anything that is doing "being" that can switch it on or off?

Describe what you notice.

Sending love.

Friederich: Dear Ilona, Wow! That's so great! Thank you. The "sense of me" is definitely growing less, even since yesterday's e-mail. I read the first chapter of your book and came to a point where the question arose, *Why the heck did I write her so desperately yesterday? It's really no big deal!* Or, is that just a "strategy to avoid the seeing of no me?" We will see.

I'm finding it hard even to find a "sense of me." It seems to be something showing up, appearing, and disappearing as a temporary "thing"—a part of *what is.* When it seems to appear, it is sensed as surrounding and including the body, with a sense of being and aliveness, which is just here quietly, simply present. If the "sense of me" is given a different name—say that it's labeled "broccoli"—then it doesn't feel personal anymore: it's just seen as a thing—neutral—and more space is experienced.

No, definitely, a sense of being isn't happening "to me" but *is* "me"! Without thinking or thoughts, there is definitely only is-ness...*being.* It lasts only a fraction of a second, and then all thoughts are back. And no, the sense of being isn't personal; it's simply something that is—and in a way, it feels like this "sense of being" would be, sort of, the real "me." And no: there isn't anything doing being. Being is simply *what is.*

But then, for some reason, a "sucking in" seems to happen, an identification with thoughts, emotions, and sensations with a story. Then aliveness seems gone, and eternal hell seems to be back. When

I wrote "for some reason," that wasn't completely accurate. Most of the time, the "sucking in" is triggered by some outside event.

This unit called Friederich has been built with a rather intolerant personality, which makes it almost impossible to live with other people. Add to that a paralysis from the neck downwards for more than thirty-four years, and because of the last five years spent lying in bed for most of the day and night some very resistant bedsores in both of its buttocks, and you get an idea of how "perfectly" it is all scripted! LOL! I mean, it's like, *Change or suffer and die! Realize your true nature or you will keep suffering.*

Thank you for your willingness to support me on this adventure, and to dedicate some of your time to this nonexistent "me"! Or, more accurate yet, to the bursting the bubble of the nonexistent "me"!

The next day...

Friederich: Ilona—knowing how committed you are to support others in seeing clearly, and having no answer from you yet, I suspect that maybe, for whatever reason, you are not getting my e-mail. So, I am sending it here again, hoping that this time it will land in your mailbox! Thank you.

Ilona: Hi Friederich. Thank you for your e-mail; indeed the message got lost and it's good that you sent it again yesterday. I normally reply in a day or two. If I don't, it's either because I'm very busy or something did not reach me.

You can write to me every day, this way the mind gets to focus and clarifies what is going on. This process is yours, so just write what you notice, what is going on, even if I don't reply to every e-mail.

What you wrote about being rings true. Yes, being just is. The sense of me is not constant. It arises and passes away within situations. The sense of me is not even a sense of me, but a contraction, plus labels that say "me."

For a day, examine the language and how it is constructed. We have a subject/object doing action.

Notice "I" breathe—does that make "I" the breather or is it a way to describe breathing happening?

I lie in bed—is it "I" that is laying?

The computer sits on a table—is there a computer doing sitting?

There is an exercise for you on my blog called "Labels," do it here or on paper and notice how language creates an illusion of doer [see page 76 in this book].

Answer the questions from the post, plus tell me, how does the labeling experience affect actual experience? How does labeling what is happening affect what is happening?

Sending love.

Friederich: Thank you, Ilona! You not getting my e-mail was a good opportunity for insight because a lot of old patterns of, apparently, not being good enough and being rejected came up, and the belief that the story is true happened again! Depression, resentment, and anger arose again and were experienced as "I" am that anger, that resentment, that depression. Until the identification with the story was seen through again, especially after the last e-mail was sent to you!

Reading the exercise recommended by you, and other posts on your website about the myth of permanent enlightenment, helped seeing more clearly that whatever is, is. If permanent enlightenment happens, then so be it. If getting caught up in the story and believing it happens again, then so be it. If it happens over and over again, then so be it. Anyway, it's just another story.

So then, this is what came up in the twenty-minute exercise:

> I'm lying in bed, dictating this text. I'm doing my best to speak very clearly so that my dictation device can write exactly what

I'm dictating, and not write some errors. At the same time, I'm thinking thoughts about worrying about making mistakes, getting stirred up by noises people around me could make which would negatively affect my dictations. Hence, the accuracy of my dictation. I'm trying to breathe slowly in order to avoid tension. I'm getting nervous and anxious because I'm hearing the neighbors moving around and making noise, which could affect the quality of my dictations because the software can't differentiate between my voice and other noises. Hence, everything gets (in a way) translated into words! Which for me is very annoying and makes me very angry and feeling like a victim! I'm waiting for the next thing to write, but nothing comes up. I'm looking at the clock and still have two minutes to go! I would rather wake up once and forever instead of doing these kinds of exercises! I'm tired of the whole shit!

Laying in bed is happening as well as speaking into the microphone so that the dictation device can transcribe the spoken words into written words. Listening to the river is happening as well as breathing. Anger is rising because of the inability to pronounce the word "breathing" (the dictation device always understands it as "briefing"). A desire for "perfection" is here, a judgement that says "what is" isn't perfect, but something else would be instead. Laying in bed is noticed as well as thoughts and emotions coming and going. Waiting for the nurse is also noticed, as well as a certain lightness and slight joy about the day. Watching the clock is noticed as well as two more minutes and liking to complete the ten-minute exercise! It is seen that describing what happens and *what is* in this way feels much lighter and smoother, more flowing, whereas the traditional way feels harder, "cut out," like, "cemented in."

So, it seems that there would be a choice in both ways of living. Describing what life is seems to be equally "valuable"— because both of them appear to exist—and the second way of seeing definitely feels much more gentle and soft.

Who knows? Maybe there is a purpose behind a "slow" awakening instead of a spontaneous and permanent one! I mean, the only one having a preference in this, wouldn't that be the illusionary "I"? LOL! Isn't everything already exactly the way it is supposed to be? Even the apparent "I," "believing" the story to be his or her story? Who or what is it anyway that is identifying itself with the I-thought? Isn't that infinite aliveness itself, since there is nothing else?!

It seems that if awakening isn't spontaneous and permanent, great alertness and commitment is needed. Alertness and commitment in sticking to the "non-me" narration of what is instead of the "I" narration. If it is seen that everything is really only happening without a me doing it or making it happen, then there is immediate ease and smoothness present.

It is clearly seen that without labeling, there would be only presence, no experiencing. As soon as language comes in, labeling starts. Even in such subtle forms as naming things by their name, experiencing kicks in and, of course, even more so when labeling experiences and emotions as good and bad, right and wrong, enjoyable not enjoyable, liking or not liking.

It seems that there is no way to stop this from happening. Labeling/wording just appears to happen with no one doing it.

Thanks for your time!

And for your love!

Ilona: Thank you for the reply, Friederich. You can trust that all is unfolding as it should. Seeing no self is not enlightenment, it's a first step, crossing a line, the beginning of the awakened journey. It is not a door to happily ever after, it's a door to the exploration of what this is.

Seeing that there is no one here, no entity, clears the want for enlightenment, as it is seen that there is no one here to achieve that. The whole story of enlightenment can no longer find a place that can stick. No more seeking, but exploration does not end.

Okay. Let's dig deeper. Yes, you see it, labeling is just happening without a doer.

Now, focus on the narration, the voice in the head. Let it talk in whatever way it wants to talk and take a look:

What is there that is listening to it?

What is that voice talking to/at?

Is it always telling the truth?

What is it arguing with?

What is there that cares?

Which story is the voice engaged in?

Have a look. Is there a me, or a story *about* me?

Is there Friederich, or a story *about* Friederich?

Does the voice in the head know anything?

What is it that knows of this voice?

Looking forward to your answers. Sending love.

Friederich: Dear Ilona, Thanks!

Seeing that there is no one here, no entity, clears the want for enlightenment, as it is seen that there is no one here to achieve that. The whole story of enlightenment can no longer find a place that can stick. No more seeking, but exploration does not end.

It seems here there is still a "curiosity" to explore more.

What is that voice talking to/at?

It seems as if this voice would talk to a "me" but then, upon further seeing, it also seems that there is only an awareness of that voice talking and that "I" identify with this awareness as "me." It feels lighter to just phrase it as "awareness that voice is happening."

Is it always telling the truth?

LOL, no, not at all! Actually, it is almost never telling the truth!

What is it arguing with?

Mostly, it is *against* what is in each given moment. It is *resisting* what is in each moment. It is almost never satisfied with *what is.* Apparently, his voice has "clear" ideas about how mostly everything should be in order for it to be enjoyable and "right." It has its "own" opinion about almost everything.

What is there that cares?

Which story is the voice engaged in?

That's tricky! It would seem like this awareness would have its own opinion about the opinions of the voice, but then, this can't be true because *something else is aware* of that dynamic. So, it seems rather that there is an awareness of two voices: one arguing/commenting on *what is,* and the other arguing/commenting on that first voice!

"I" seems more identified with the latter one than with the former. What is also interesting is that I pay that much attention to the first voice! It's almost as if that voice would be an authority. Somebody once said that this voice could be compared to a "roommate" who is continuously commenting and arguing on everything. If it were a roommate, I could kick her out! LOL! "Shut up and leave me alone!" But, apparently, it isn't that easy. Unless it is—who knows!

Have a look. Is there a me, or a story about me?

Is there Friederich, or a story about Friederich?

Yes, unfortunately, there is a story *about* me. In a way, it's still all about me! This story is as hard to kick out as cockroaches! While it is more and more frequently seen that this me-story is just a story, the being sucked into the story still happens very frequently, completely on autopilot. Especially because the story is so intensely felt/linked to the body, the body is feeling it. The focus is on the bodily sensations, and that *seems* to be all that there is. But, of course, something is aware of this too! So, what if who I truly am is this awareness? And everything is just happening in that awareness? How could I "anchor" myself as this awareness, at least, more often?

Does the voice in the head know anything?

What is it that knows of this voice?

This voice knows very little! Almost nothing! Only in a few practical areas does it know anything, and it seems that almost everything it appears to know, if not totally everything, is based on past experience. Although it always tries to comment and "predict" the future, it literally has no clue, and does so mostly on past experiences. Again, "raising the dead" comes to my mind! LOL! Like I wrote before: It would seem that awareness knows of this voice. Infinite awareness appears to be aware of this voice, as well as of everything that is—I mean, without infinite awareness, we couldn't even say that something exists.

Nice questions!

Thanks—until whenever.

Ilona: Great investigation.

Have a closer look, is there more than one voice talking?

What is behind the voice?

Is it the body that experiences, or is the body, too, experienced?

Consider the voice as a radio—it keeps talking, you pay attention to content or not, the story keeps being narrated. Do you expect the story to stop being told? It's not like that. It keeps arising, but when the belief in trueness drops, so does the volume. The voice can talk away, without being judged as wrong.

Being sucked into the story happens, but what does the story stick to?

Sending love.

Friederich:

Have a closer look, is there more than one voice talking?

There doesn't seem to be a voice, but only the awareness of thoughts, and like a "process," "custom," "tendency," or "identification" (it's hard to find the exact word) to hold those thoughts as true. This happens completely automatically. There also seems to be a total and complete reliance on those thoughts, an "absolute" trust in the validity of what they are saying, like, a statement of what is. It is also seen that in times of apparent confusion, sadness, anger, depression, or "problems," thinking is used in order to bring clarity and ease, or to discern between awareness and what this awareness is aware of. Also there is an investigation of trying to find out if this awareness is affected by what it is aware of. (The insight, of course, is always no! Awareness is this still, quiet, peaceful, serene, "empty" presence.) Oftentimes, there *are*, apparently, thoughts fighting/arguing, which could refer to two different sources, but they are sensed as having the exact same quality.

What is behind the voice?

At times (very seldom), I can recognize my father's belief system behind the voices, and other times I can recognize that a "teacher" would have said that. Most of the time, there isn't anything recognized behind those thoughts; they just seem to arise, and disappear again. Sometimes they seem to arise over and over and over and over again. You get the point! LOL!

Is it the body that experiences, or is the body, too, experienced?

No; the body doesn't appear to experience anything, it just appears to happen *in* the body (the contraction, the pain, the joy, the pleasure, the warm, the cold), which then seems to be owned by an illusionary "me" as "my" pain, "my" sadness; "I am feeling joyful, sad"; "I am depressed, angry"; and so forth. Like I said before, this all seems to happen completely on autopilot.

Consider the voice as a radio—it keeps talking, you pay attention to content or not, the story keeps being narrated.

There, that's where the problem could be. There seems to be a complete and total inability to *not* pay attention to the story being narrated. The same appears to be true for whatever sounds appear in the surroundings. It seems like something is always scanning the environment for noises/voices, and, most of the time, gets completely and totally upset by it! Actually, this seems to be one of the biggest annoyances in the story line.

And, yes, there *is* a very, very high expectation for the story to be stopped from being told. This would seem like heaven!

I hear what you are saying about that (stopping of the story) not being so, and that by not believing it, it weakens. I first learned about that in late 2001, with Byron Katie: "Is it true?" And despite having done "The Work" diligently over years, not much has changed (if anything). Since I'm using a dictation device in order to write (which I have to, because of the physical limitations), this scanning the surroundings for possible noises has become even more extreme because the dictation device can't differentiate between what I am dictating and other noises. It reacts to both! LOL—grrr!!! (Thoughts/feelings of victimhood and rage are coming up!) I would truly love to be able to be more effective in seeing through the lies and the stories! And even if on a conscious level I am very clear about the illusory appearances of the story, "something deep down" (unconscious) still appears to hold on/believe in those stories! *Help!*

Instead of simply seeing through the story, I fight it, like *Go away! You are not true!* Which, of course, holds it in place! How to cut this vicious cycle?!

Being sucked into the story happens, but what does the story stick to?

I have no clue. At times I sensed that it was as if something wouldn't allow me to be free from the story, which I know isn't true, and that I can only do this to myself. This "something wouldn't allow me to be free from the story" is just another belief—seeing as an appearance in awareness—but it seems a very sticky one. There seems to be another belief, like "That would be too much freedom!" As if that would make me too different or bigger than all the "other" people. Sometimes, even something like I haven't earned it yet, to be that free. Guilt? Another thought: I never get what I truly want, and even if I do get it, it's usually never what I thought it would give me.

If it was talking only positive stuff, would that too be a problem? Positive stuff in the usual sense, would be a problem as well. Constructive stuff like "What if it is not true?" or "Who knows if that is the case?" would be no problem.

I have begun thanking the inner voice and there is a shift experienced (although, not as thoroughly as desired/expected, LOL. Of course, that thought can be thanked also!).

Funny. It seems like the deeper the going, the tougher, more intense it gets, and, at the same time, also easier and faster!

Thank us!

Ilona: Great investigation!

"Me" cannot get rid of the story; it's the same as Batman. Batman cannot get rid of the story about Batman. It's all a story.

Try this:

Remember something from the past. For a minute hold an image of the event, something significant.

Tell me, is this story the same if you are in a good mood or a bad mood?

Do other people remember it the same way?

Is there a true story?

Is this story owned by you?

How does the story appear?

When does it appear?

Is it possible to change what happened?

Is it possible to change the story about what happened?

Examine this closely.

Then for a minute imagine yourself in two years' time.

Can you see that image being created?

Focus on here now. Let this *what is* be okay.

Is there much story in the present?

How are the story and time connected?

These are questions for you, dear Friederich. Have fun with them. Looking forward to answers. Sending love.

Friederich: Hi Ilona!

"Me" cannot get rid of the story; it's the same as Batman. Batman cannot get rid of the story about Batman. It's all a story.

Excellent observation. Once it is seen, *so* obvious!

Remember something from the past.

Although the basic story line is the same, the sensations and details vary each time I remember that story. Of course other people won't necessarily remember the exact same story. If we are lucky, we might get some agreements on what it is that is remembered. Most likely, though, the meaning and significance of the story are for each person going to be different, if not very different.

Is there a true story?

It would depend on how you define "true." If "true" is what is at each moment, and for each person, then yes, there would be a *true* story.

But, if what you mean by "true story" is the actual facts and what was really going on, you can forget the notion of a true story. All we have are just stories.

Is the story owned by me? When seeing clearly: no, it is just a story and anybody could own it. LOL.

The story appears to arise spontaneously all by itself. It does just appear and sometimes it appears to stay even for quite some time. Other times it disappears right away. There could be something happening that could trigger the story. It is never possible to change what happened because what happened, happened. Although, another story would gladly insist that what happened could have been different. That's a lie. Is it possible to change the story about what happened? Yes. Thank goodness. This happens all the time, and a lot of times rather naturally. Like we have seen before, how something appears to be "remembered." Oftentimes it depends from where (from what emotional state) it is remembered. Also, most of the time, seeing what supposedly has happened takes out at least some of the apparent intensity.

On another note: How can I truly, truly, truly *know* that something is remembered and not just a story that shows up, which has another story of "this has happened in the past" attached to it?

Then for a minute imagine yourself in two years' time.

Can you see that image being created?

Yes, I can see that image being imagined, out of nothing, or maybe out of conditioning, with all its likes or don't likes, with all its expectations.

Focus on here now. Let this what is be okay.

Is there much story in the present?

No—no thoughts, no story. The story seems to arise again whenever something appears to occur that isn't welcomed. For example, right now when the neighbor is starting to cut his grass precisely when I'm dictating. Besides that, I just don't like that noise. I like silence, quietness, which of course is also just a story.

How are the story and time connected?

Of course, the story needs time. Maybe, the story *is* time. They seem to be one and the same.

Thank you, Ilona, for playing with me.

Ilona: Brilliant. You are digging right in! Sweet.

On another note: How can I truly, truly, truly know *that something is remembered and not just a story that shows up, which has another story of "this has happened in the past" attached to it?*

Memory comes up as a familiar image with the story. Sensations, feelings are involved; it's a rich experience of a story. All you can know is that it's a story about the past, a story about imagined events with a different flavor.

What is here now—this *is* what is happening. Memory is a story about what is *not* happening right now. So is future—a story about what is not happening.

Have a look: can you find a container of stored stories?

Did I ask you to watch Alan Watts's video? You can look it up on YouTube: Alan Watts's "boat analogy" [see the video at https://www.youtube.com/watch?v=G4j6cUwCRmI]. It's brilliant how he illustrates time.

The key is to recognize a story as a story.

Can you choose which stories are being told by the voice in the head?

Does it matter?

Sending love.

Friederich:

Can you find a container of stored stories?

Yes! And that container is located in Fort Knox, and traded at Wall Street, LOL. Of course, there isn't any container of stored stories; maybe at best we could say that they all arise out of Infinite Consciousness. No thing.

Can you choose which stories are being told by the voice in the head?

Tricky question! It seems that it would depend: In general the story just seems to arise, but it would seem that I could focus on what kind of story I would like if I choose to focus. So in this sense, it would seem that I could choose to imagine a horror story or a love story, but from where or from what would that choice come? From where or from what would all the imagined details come? It would seem that as long as the story "I" am able to imagine is to my liking, I would easily say: "I imagine that story." Whereas if the story is less pleasing I might say: "That story just arose."

Does it matter?

For this unit here, it still does matter. I would prefer an interesting story over a story of ugliness, war, horror, cruelty, or the like. For example, I would rather prefer to walk again, and to do all the things I did back then, than lie in bed as I'm doing now. What if this preference comes from *what is* or from the *I am that?* I mean, where else could *anything* come from? And, is this not who *I truly am?*

Hugs to You.

Ilona:

In general, the story just seems to arise, but it would seem…

The word "seems" means that I haven't checked something out yet, it equals "illusion." It *seems* like, but is this the case in actuality?

In actuality, do you choose which story plays in the head?

The story "I can choose any story" is another story. Is that story true?

If you really could choose any story, would this story be the one being repeated over and over again?

The key is to see that stories are stories, not reality. Stories arise, and if emotional reaction is triggered, it can quickly escalate into full-blown drama. Thoughts come charged with emotions, more emotions trigger more thoughts, and here you go—madness!

Yes, you are in bed, not running around. If you resist this situation there is suffering. The only way out is through acceptance. Accepting this as it is fully without any "but."

The journey of awakening is a journey of acceptance, surrender. The first thing to accept is the resistance itself. Reaction to a story is what keeps it going. Reaction of resistance. Resisting *what is*.

Without accepting resistance as a valid experience, we cannot move forward. Resistance is a friend: it's showing the way into what else needs to be accepted.

So for a few minutes, feel your situation, feel it fully. Feel resistance and let *all* just be okay. Just for a couple of minutes, allow this to be okay as it is. If you can, welcome it all and bow in honor, thanking this. Keep at it for a bit.

See what happens.

Sending love.

Friederich: Well, in the way it is seen from here, I like to, whenever possible, let the doors open for something else. That I may, right now, not be able to see. From where I am right now, all that I can say is that I have absolutely *no* idea from where thoughts arise. At the very same time, there is also a feeling sense that it is *all me*. If I am truly all that is, then in some very mysterious way (that I have no clue as of yet, and maybe never will) I must be the authority on all thoughts and decisions, as well as all *that is*! I mean, there isn't anybody else! Of course, it's not the person. It's like when Jesus supposedly said, "I and my father are one." That's why I also trust that all these desires to walk again, travel, play the accordion again, take photographs, ski, and so forth are there *for a reason*. Even if I would still identify myself with the person, those thoughts or desires would be there *for a reason*.

As far as I can see, this life, this universe, is not a senseless and purposeless creation/dream. Just because I can't see exactly what that reason really is, it doesn't mean that there isn't one. I also sense that the story is there for a reason. Probably just for fun. In a way, this entire dream seems like a giant and brilliant story factory to me! At one point, it may be seen that this is all BS, but at the time I sense that this point of view really supports me, that I could focus on what kind of story I would like if I choose to focus, so in this sense, it would seem that I could choose to imagine a horror story or a love story. Of course, from where or from what would that choice come? From where or from what would all the imagined details come? It would seem that as long as the story "I am able to imagine" is of my liking, I easily could say: "I imagine that story!" Whereas that story to the left I would then say, "That story just arose."

In actuality, do you choose which story plays in the head?

The story "I can choose any story" is another story. Is that story true?

When I woke up from a six-day coma last year (without any near-death experience), the first thing I remembered was a very intense and angry discussion about *Who the fuck is driving the bus here?* The next thing I remembered was that "something/somebody" presented me with a question: *Do you want to stay here (in this dream) or do you want to leave it?* I heard the sound of rain and "decided" to stay here. I am aware that in order to choose one over the other, there must be a preference already set. Otherwise, how could I prefer one thing over another?! What put that preference there, and how it came there, I have no idea.

The way I see it at times, it can be very constructive to assume that there would be free will, but at other times it is more constructive to accept that there isn't. For example, if I ask "What else is possible?"—or "What are the infinite possibilities for this body to show up as completely healed?"—I could say that those questions just show up, as well as the possible options. It could also be that nothing will show up, who knows? And, no, I have absolutely no choice in what story is playing in my head, it even would seem that I have absolutely no choice if something makes me become aware of the story playing, or if I'm just seduced by the story. Yes, it's a sweet story that I have, at times, sort of, free will—LOL!

If you really could choose any story, would this story be the one being repeated over and over again?

No, no story is good enough to be repeated over and over again in my head. If I could choose, I would choose no story!

Reaction to a story is what keeps it going. Reaction of resistance. Resisting what is.

Yes, I came to see this beautifully today. Resistance is a friend. Beautiful! This is something else I also came to see today more clearly. I seldom use the word "but," because it's a complete negation of what I said/wrote before I introduced that word. I prefer "and"— like "Okay, I'm in bed now, *and* what else is possible?" It's like the saying that goes, "What you resist, persists." And what else is possible?

So for a few minutes, feel your situation, feel it fully. Feel resistance and let all just be okay. Just for a couple of minutes allow this to be okay as it is. If you can, welcome it all and bow in honor, thanking this.

Sweet, *sweet, sweeet!*

Thank you so much, Ilona! These inquiries are priceless! Like the commercials go, and for everything else, use the MasterCard. LOL.

Friederich: Dear Ilona, In my excitement, I forgot to tell you how the little exercise went. While being with the resistance, I suddenly remembered a process I learned about fourteen years ago that's called "Core Transformation."

So, I ask that resistance, "What is it that you want to get by resisting?" Surprisingly, it said, *I want to ensure that you get out of bed.* LOL! It was so beautiful because I could clearly see how utterly innocent that part was. A very honorable intention, but, completely useless. What is so beautiful about it is the fact that the intention was utterly *good—loving*!

I did the same with the intolerance of noise. When I asked, "What is it that you want to achieve with this anger towards noise?" The answer was, *Peace.* When I dug further, asking, "If you have total and complete peace, all the time, no matter what, what is it that you would like to achieve through that?" The answer was, *Being.* Just amazing being, no matter what!

It was so beautiful to realize that, no matter the appearance (anger, resistance), the underlying (misdirected) intention is always good! Loving! So, I feel deep appreciation for you having pointed those inquiries out to me! Big hug!

Ilona: Nice! Yes, all is love, sometimes in disguise. It is one thing to see that separate self is illusion, it's another thing to say yes to whatever comes up.

Say yes to lying in bed. Accept that as it is. Surrender to this.

See if there is something that wants to escape this situation. Say yes to that too, and let this be okay. See what is behind it. And deeper, and deeper. Till you are seeing that situation as it is, perfect for you *as it is*. Rest in that. Sending love.

Friederich: Accepting what is, and surrendering to it, feels right and light—and how can that happen? I have no clue about how to accomplish that.

Some things seem easy to accept while some others, not so much. Some others, impossible. There is something that is just plain denying it. For example, I've been lying in bed for more than five years (except for a few months, when I could sit in the wheelchair). My argument goes like this: "It's already challenging having to live life with a paralyzed body, that's enough for one lifetime! And now, having to accept lying in bed also? No way!" Especially so when this lying in bed happens in a surrounding that has very noisy music all day and all night. I sense that I have the right to at least lie in bed in a quiet and peaceful place! This is plain torture! No human being should ever have to live that way! Why should any human being have to live in something it just doesn't like? That's insane! Even if I could accept and surrender to this torture, for what good would that be?

How could that be love?! I have no plans to play Jesus or, for that matter, another martyr! As I see it, that time is over! I don't think that spirituality or non-duality is to be taken that way! Or am I wrong?! If there truly is no me (which I haven't found) why not just take this body out of circulation (life)? Why endure all this torture just to have the same experience a few days, months, or years later?

I'm aware that this is a very fierce e-mail, and (just in case, but I'm pretty sure you won't) it's not personal. I'm just desperate! Since I'm living in this noisy country (Colombia), I'm trying to be at peace with noise. I have moved places countless times, and thanks to progress (electricity being brought to remote places, sound equipment cheaper and more powerful), the noise always reaches me again. Relentless. It seems like the more I enjoy stillness and quietness, the noisier my environment gets. And, since I have to lie in bed, I can't escape it!

I know you don't have one, but just in case you do: a magic bullet?

Thanks for reading this far, Ilona!

Ilona:

Accepting what is, and surrendering to it, feels right and light—and how can that happen? I have no clue about how to accomplish that.

It's not an accomplishment, it's giving up trying.

Some things seem easy to accept while some others, not so much. Some others, impossible.

Yes, I know what you mean. But once again, the awakening journey is about surrender. All that is showing up is already accepted on the deepest level. It is here because of all the conditions and circumstances. If it's happening, it's exactly what should be happening. How to know that? It's already here.

Yes, there is a huge resistance to what is happening. Can you accept that this resistance is here and just let it be here for a few minutes? Feel it fully and allow it fully.

Then look behind it, what is there? What is resisting *what is*? What needs to be protected by this resistance?

I'm aware that this is a very fierce e-mail, and (just in case, but I'm pretty sure you won't) it's not personal. I'm just desperate!

Yes, it is a fierce expression, and it is an honest one. All good. What needs to be expressed is allowed and welcomed. There is anger and fear, there is desperation. It's okay to feel as you feel.

But look behind, what is behind the sensations?

Yeah, I can imagine the noise and frustration. There is something to look at here too. What is trying to escape the noise?

I know you don't have one, but just in case you do: a magic bullet?

Ha ha, nope, I have no magic bullet, only red pills. Sending you love. Keep digging, you are getting close.

Friederich: There is great mastery in resisting whatever is, and an absolute cluelessness about how to be open and accepting of whatever is.

Although I would say that there is total and complete willingness to let go of resistance of *what is*, a clear recognition of the total and complete insanity of resisting *what is* (because it is already existing), at the same time, there is also complete and utter powerlessness over the process of letting go.

There is an immense desire to let go of resistance because it is so clearly seen that there are only two choices: completely letting go of resistance and being at peace and happy (maybe even able to marvel and celebrate *what is*), or to resist *what is* and suffer immeasurable pain, including physical pain.

At least there is a loving recognition of the innocence of this resistance; from its point of view, it is trying to protect me, and give me peace. It just does not work at all! Any clue? Any probing questions?

Thanks, Ilona.

Ilona: Yes, it is total insanity. It all already is. So you can bang your head against the wall and be upset about it or just say, "Hmm, I wonder, what else is here that can be looked at and just watched."

You are seeing it, resistance is pointless. And yet it is here. Accept resistance and thank it for doing such a great job.

Can you see that resistance is a friend? If not, have a look.

Bow to it in honor. Notice the mechanism is working perfectly.

From its point of view, it is trying to protect me, and give me peace. It just does not work at all!

If it is not helping, is there a need to keep resisting? Keep writing every day! Sending love.

Friederich: What drives me most crazy is the fact that if I could push a button and all the resistance would be gone, I would. The problem (or maybe a blessing in disguise) is that it doesn't matter if I would rather give up resisting or not, it is still there! It doesn't care about my vote. It feels like I have absolutely no say in this. I'm feeling like an endlessly punished or "tested" puppet! Don't I have already enough by being paralyzed, and having to lie in bed? Do I really have to deal with all this resistance also?

Is this what this character's life is all about—completely and totally senseless and useless struggle, "working" on giving up resistance without succeeding? How absolutely pointless!

"Unfair" comes to my mind! While other people are having fun, this character is utterly, hopelessly struggling to just give up resisting! This predicament is so utterly pointless that it almost makes me laugh! (No wonder people came up with karma and working up past life's sin! LOL!)

It reminds me of the year and a half I participated in ayahuasca sessions. Almost every fifteen days, I asked for unconditional love to be shown. I got unconditional hell! Interestingly enough, each following session, there was absolutely no effect from the ayahuasca. Not a slightest physiological or psychological alteration! Like if I would have drunk a strong tea, it didn't even matter how much I drank! But the following time, oh boy, oh boy! Never saw something, just felt horrible guilt and despair for almost two hours, then it faded slowly away (but, as I see it now, with no actual *dissolving* of those patterns).

Can you see that resistance is a friend? If not, have a look.

No. I can't! I see it rather as something that is standing in the way (quite pointless and useless, may I say) to my peace and happiness! I rather feel like a completely senseless and unfairly, cruelly punished victim!

What is behind resistance? I have no clue. This is another point that drives me crazy! You are asking me on and on what is "behind"! And, all that comes up is *nothing*! (It's not nothing as much as *no thing*. I just don't see anything.)

If it is not helping, is there a need to keep resisting?

No, but the "problem" is that it is not something I am doing, it's something that is just happening like the weather!

Will there ever be an end to this? While I can truly see that resistance has lessened regarding a lot of issues, there simply seems to be a never-ending supply of other issues. It's almost like Pandora's box!

Thank you for reading and letting me pour out!

Ilona: That is only unfair if you are the character. But, are you the character?

The way I see it, love has many forms and shapes. It is not just a happy, joyful, expanded feeling, it is also the deepest, darkest, most horrible hole. It is everything. The intensity of feeling (whatever is being felt) is the intensity of love.

Love burns through all conditioning. If it is showing up as darkness, that too is love, in disguise. It too is a gift. Unconditional love is unbound, it's what is being felt with no conditions.

The love that you seek is your own love for yourself.

Love is not what you think. It's what you feel. Including thousands of its shapes and forms. In the end it's all about loving *what is*. The relationship with *what is* equals love manifesting. If you are saying no to reality, love feels like resistance, like tension, suffering. Can you see what I'm saying?

The heart wants to love, freely and openly.

The mind is guarding it from being hurt. The mind is protecting the heart. The conflict is that the mind sets conditions. Trying to fit love into what is acceptable and what is not. Love is too big for that. So it hurts.

What is behind resistance? I have no clue. This is another point that drives me crazy! You are asking me on and on what is "behind"! And, all that comes up is nothing! *(It's not nothing as much as* no thing. *I just don't see anything.)*

Yes! Nothing. Nothing at all. Good that you see that! It's not the absence of the answer. It is the answer. There is nothing there. At all.

How does that make you feel?

It is not something I am doing, it's something that is just happening like the weather!

The pattern is here till it isn't.

Once the hole in the system is punctured, there is a collapsing time and cleanup time. So be patient and notice that there is something happening. There is no control over it. So just watch it unfold. Enjoy the ride, if you can. Sending love.

Friederich:

That is only unfair if you are the character. But, are you the character?

At times, there is less identification with a character, and at other times, there is more. If the wind machine is relatively quiet or peaceful, it is easier to just watch it. At all times, rather full identification is going on.

What if you are not able to see hell as a gift? Is it still a gift? To whom?

Unconditional love is unbound, it's what is being felt with no conditions.

If "unconditional love" would be present, wouldn't that be the end of hell and suffering?!

The love that you seek is your own love for yourself.

Sounds true. The question is, how to see that?!

In the end it's all about loving what is.

Yeah: I know. Byron Katie, that's just so that she hated her life and everything else, with all her heart, until awakening happened, and she was gone! [Byron Katie, author of the book *Loving What Is*, describes her experience before awakening as being full of hate for her life. Once she awakened, she fell deeply in love with *what is*.] After that, yes, she had to go through feelings of intense guilt and shame and so on—who doesn't?! It's rather easy to "love *what is*" when you play in the sunshine!

Yes, I can see what you are saying, and like I wrote above, who wouldn't "love *what is*" if you are playing in the sunshine, or at least if your mind patterns/psychological patterns are not causing you any major troubles! But what about when you have been living in hell for forty years? Except for a few days of sunshine, and then you think, *Oh, my goodness, I think something really shifted finally for the better!* just to be back in hell a few days later. Honestly, this is one of the cruellest way of having to "live"! Talk about the perfect torture!

Trying to fit love into what is acceptable and what is not.

So, are you saying that I better prepare myself to live for the rest of my life living in hell, and *loving* it? If that is all that is possible, I would rather take myself out of the game!

Yes! Nothing. Nothing at all. Good that you see that! It's not the absence of answer. It is the answer. There is nothing there. At all.

No, I didn't mean that. What I meant was: resistance is all that is. Resistance is it. It's all there is to life! (At least to this one.) Resistance is what life is. Period.

If it is not helping, is there a need to keep resisting?

How does that make you feel?

Unbearable! It makes "me" want to kill myself!

The pattern is here till it isn't.

Yeah, and probably it is meant not to change, so what's the point?!

Notice that there is something happening.

This is precisely the most excruciating pain-causing point! Seems that for years I'm doing one kind or another of consciousness work. While there have been some, maybe minor, shifts for the better, as you can see from my writing, the entire structure is still mostly excruciatingly painful. Like my mom said a few days ago, more patience!

Sorry, but I am not enjoying the ride! Actually, I hate it to the bottom! And besides all my best efforts, countless money and courses and books, I'm still hating it! Maybe even more, because nothing has really worked! This whole "life thing" rather feels like a huge and gigantic fraud! Like a very, very bad and mean and evil commercial for an adventure park that is advertised as being full of fun and love and laughter, and when you get there, it's the house of terror!

Life equals the most cruel thing!

Sending love.

Is this real love, or love disguised?!

Ilona: Hi, Friederich. I sense a lot of anger in your last e-mail. *Resistance is what life is?* No, man! Resistance is what arises in life as part of life when we say *no* to what is happening. Either you say yes or no—but life goes on as it did. The difference is how we feel about it. You can hate or love, it's still happening. I am repeating myself here, but I have to say it again. The only way out is *through* surrender.

Can I ask you, what is your motive for this investigation? To fix something that is not working, or to see the truth no matter what?

Are you looking for freedom from unwanted feelings? If so, it's not how it works. The freedom is to experience all, good, bad, and the ugly, without judgement that it's wrong. The key is to realize that shoulds and should nots are the very things that make for a distorted view.

Unconditional love knows no conditions and it will break through, burn through, all limitations.

Write to me what you expect should be happening?

What do you want to happen?

What do you expect should change?

Sending love.

Friederich:

The only way out is through *surrender.*

And, what's adding even more frustration is, at least in my experience, it doesn't matter if I say yes or no because life keeps on being exactly the same! In a way, even saying yes to whatever appears to happen comes out of a wish for things to ease, to cool down—at least as far as possible—the heat since late '99. I have come to see that only through unconditional love can suffering end. But, no success regarding being able to love unconditionally. It only adds more anger and frustration to what already is. So then, can I at least let go of trying to unconditionally love? No! Not a chance! Can I at least just let go of the whole thing and stop adding any layers to it through thinking? No! Not a chance! It all seems to happen automatically—even trying to accept or plainly reject.

Can I ask you, what is your motive for this investigation? To fix something that is not working, or to see the truth no matter what?

"Truth" seems to be too fancy a word. I do want peace and serenity, no matter what, to be at ease, no matter what.

Are you looking for freedom from unwanted feelings?

Yes! This is exactly what I want! Well then, what's the point in investigating?! So the anger is okay, the hatred is okay, the disability is okay, the hell is okay? So why do this investigation? Oh, okay! This investigation is also just what is happening, and it doesn't have to lead to liberation or whatever we want to call it! It doesn't matter what we do or not do; except when it does, and then something appears to change because of what apparently has been done or not, but that's just another story!

Unconditional love knows no conditions and it will break through, burn through, all limitations.

You see? There you put the carrot again right in front of me! So then, I truly want unconditional love with all my heart—unconditional love! Because, if there is one thing I want over all others, it is this: to break through all limitations! I mean: If I am able to love whatever is, there can't be any suffering at all!

Write to me what you expect should be happening.

What do you want to happen?

What do you expect should change?

What I want to happen is a true opening to unconditional love! What I don't want happening is to keep all this hatred and fear and anger going on! I want the misery to end! Once and for all! I'm working on this now for over fourteen years! It's about time!

Thank you, Ilona.

And, Ilona, I experience these experiences of going down into hell periodically—about every two weeks. They are always very intense, like *I can't handle this anymore! Take me out, please, please, please!* I never, ever, sensed that, no matter what I did, even if it was just "watching" the whole scenery unfolding, did it help the nightmare pass. It all seems to pass by itself.

Ilona: Yes, dear Friederich, it comes up and passes all by itself. Many traditions have a good mantra—"This too shall pass"—and that is useful sometimes.

Peace is always here, underneath all thinking. Suffering is story, made up of thoughts of what should be different.

Can you notice that?

Have a look, is physical pain and suffering the same?

What is in the way of feeling love now?

Friederich: Yes, some things pass, and some not. Hopefully, with death, everything has passed.

Yes, peace is always here, it's just that, very often, identification with thoughts happens to be so strong that nothing else seems possible to be here.

No, I most often sense physical pain, and it doesn't bother me, hence, no suffering! Suffering = story.

What is in the way of feeling love now?

Thinking, and physical noise! I know that that is a lie also, but I have no clue about how to feel love—even with no physical noise! Thank you, Ilona.

Ilona: *Yes!* Suffering is a story about suffering. And that story is believed, so it creates self-feeding loops to strengthen the story and triggers more feeling.

We can have a session of Deep Looking if you like. It seems to help to get to the root of the resistance mechanisms and release old patterns. It takes around an hour or more.

Friederich: Yes, I would love that!

Ilona: Sorry for the temporary disappearance, all the Christmas things got in the way of my correspondences.

We can have a session, but not today, as we have guests coming. Tomorrow would be perfect. Let me know what times are good for you. You will need an hour or two of undisturbed time. Do you know how to use any of the online chat formats? Warm regards.

Friederich: Did Santa take you for a ride?! LOL! It's all good. Tomorrow would be perfect.

Some time after the Deep Looking session…

Friederich: Hi Ilona! I'm doing fine, thank you for asking!

I had my, so far, "usual" weekend visit to hell, but the coming out of it was quick and rather easy, and the opening to more of *what is*, is even bigger! How does it get any better than this?

Since the session review, it seems way easier to be clear that thoughts showing up are just that: thoughts showing up, like crazy ghosts, flirting for my attention. It has become easier and easier to just watch them, and recognize that they are just what is showing up, but there is no need to hold them for the truth—there is no need to follow them, and believe them! Thank you! All the truly best to you.

Ilona: That is so great to hear! Looks like the door to acceptance has been opened. Yes, intense emotions come up, but pass quickly; this too is my experience. They don't stick for long and are welcomed to pass through.

Awesome. Now we can carry on looking; is I-thought any different? Is there something in experience that I-thought points to? Sending love.

Friederich: I wouldn't speak of an "I," but rather of an Is-ness/ presence, and "I" is just used to refer to it. Thank you for your love! I'm happy that you are love! Thank you!

Oh, I noticed that I resent almost everyone and everything, also a huge amount of envy! Unfairness! So, I started just to wish and imagine all those people I resented to be truly, truly happy in the way they most likely would wish it. It has been and is a truly amazing, heart-opening experience! To say the least! Thank you for knowing me.

Ilona: Wow, that is quite a turnaround, isn't it?

Can you say that it's clear, that separate entity "I" is an illusion?

Is presence the doer and thinker?

Is there a doer and thinker, a decision maker?

How would you answer that?

Friederich: Yes, it just does *appear* as if there is a separate entity! Thinking and doing, again, just happens.

Is there a doer and thinker, a decision maker?

No, it all just happens, and as this is happening, an illusory decision maker can also appear, but is seen, in the end, just as an appearance (very convincing though).

Ilona: Can you say that you are ready for the final questions, or is there still something we can look at before you are comfortable to say a big *yes?*

Friederich: LOL! If I would know what this "final question" is, I would be able to answer your question about me being ready, with absolute certainty. But, I'm sure ready for whatever questions you have for me. Is that okay with you? Sending love also! And fun!

Ilona: Ha ha, sweet! Here they are. Please answer in full, when ready, what feels true.

Much love. Have fun with this.

Friederich:

1. Is there a separate entity "self," "me," "I" at all, anywhere, in any way, shape, or form? Was there ever?

There are clouds in the sky, and at some time back, the sky seemed to identify itself with one of those clouds, and, may I say, an everchanging cloud. Now it is seen that there is only sky with clouds (thoughts, ideas, emotions, sensations, smells, tastes, and so forth) appearing, out of nowhere, and disappearing, to nowhere.

2. Explain in detail what the illusion of separate self is, when it starts, and how it works from your own experience. Describe it fully as you see it now.

When it starts? No idea! Supposedly, at the age of two to three years, but no memory of this at present. What is it? The way it is seen here is that, for whatever reason, awareness (the sky) attaches and identifies itself to/with an I-thought, together with a bunch of other thoughts (gender, family, nation, body, skills, defects, and so forth) and, somehow, convinces itself that it is all those attributes. It's like taking on a role, and so fully identifying itself with that role, that it really is able to convince itself that it is this character, while completely forgetting that all this is just brilliant and awesome appearances. This character, oftentimes, also tends to identify itself with other appearances, like houses, cars, tech toys, gadgets, and whatever objects are appearing in this awareness.

3. How does it feel to see this? What is the difference from before you started this dialogue? Please report from the past few days.

It actually feels very light and joyful. Before I could more clearly see this, there was an intellectual understanding. The identification with all the stuff going on was still very strong. Now it has lessened, although, at times, there still is a little tendency to identify with "heavy" stuff going on, but it is rather quickly seen as just "ghosts." There is also a tendency to enjoy more whatever is going on, even in what had previously been judged as harsh events/circumstances— laughter and a joyful playing attitude are more present.

4. What was the last bit that pushed you over? What made you look?

Funny enough, it was actually (last Sunday) a Skype "clearing session" with a non-duality teacher—the funny thing was that I was letting it rip, venting all my venom, and he wanted to guide me to see, but, for whatever reason, I just felt it right to put it all out! After that, it was clearly seen that this was just a storm in a water glass and... so what!

5. Do you decide, intend, choose, control events in life? Do you make anything happen? Give examples from your experience.

There is still, at times, a "pushing" towards certain things getting done, so I just go with that, while at the same time being clearer and clearer that this is just a "movement," nothing personal. I observe that I have become more thoughtful, honest, outgoing, while at the same time more accepting and loving of *what is*—hence, other characters may judge me as more self-assertive, more powerful, more going for what I want, but actually, it's all just unhindered movement. So, yes, it may appear that I would "control" more, but in fact, it's all just movement, completely appearing by itself, out of nowhere, and disappearing into nowhere.

6. Anything to add?

Another interesting thing is that there seems to be a greater certainty that this body actually will walk again, like an inner knowing, as well as the openness for those things the character wanted so badly before. But there is almost no attachment to them. It's more like "Mmh—who knows! That may actually be fun! Why not? And if not, fun and joy and laughter is anyway present!" Feels like freedom! Much appreciation! Especially for believing in me, for holding The Truth up for me!

And, *yes!* I had fun with this!

Ilona: Hi Friederich. Thank you for the answers. I can see that there is more lightness. Something changed, sweet. :)

But…

More to look at.

Is it awareness that identifies?

What is awareness?

What does it do?

Are you awareness?

(It is common to assume the position of "I am awareness," but that is not clear seeing; there is further deconstruction to do.)

Your answer to question one is not direct; can you try again, please, without metaphors?

What is "I" that goes with movement?

Is there a choice to go with movement of life or not?

Are there separate selves in other characters?

How are these other characters experienced in actuality?

I see you are very close! Keep going further! Sending love.

Friederich: No, it is the awareness that identifies. Awareness *is*, awareness is noticing. No, I am not. Awareness is. (No "I am awareness.")

Your answer to question one is not direct; can you try again, please, without metaphors?

Oooooh…and I thought I had a poetic inspiration. LOL! No, it just appeared that there was one, there was a belief, but it only was a belief, appearing to no one.

What is the "I" that goes with movement?

Is there a choice to go with movement of life or not?

Movement also just *is*. There can also be resistance to movement or just noticing movement. There can be another thought popping up of "just letting it be," a sudden thought that "resisting" hurts, letting it be equals peaceful/joyful, and this is also just noticed, by no one.

Are there separate selves in other characters?

How are these other characters experienced in actuality?

No: "They" are also just appearances; they are movements playing out. They are apparent interactions happening spontaneously; it's all just noticing, by no one.

I see you are very close! Keep going further!

"Who" is seeing "who" to be very close? Lol! Love!

Ilona: Mmm, delightful! Thank you for very clear answers.

Yeah, there is no "who."

Resistance to movement is another form of movement that arises and passes, just like everything else. Movement of thought is included.

How are you feeling these days?

Any doubt? Anything different?

If you look back at the start of this conversation, what is the most noticeable change?

What hasn't changed that you expected would change?

Sending a hug.

Friederich: Thank you, Ilona! Well, I'm feeling pretty much at ease most of the time, even joyful, for no reason. Much more relaxed about everything, even the so-called future (what will be, will be). Much more accepting of what is, including so-called others. If there isn't accepting, that's okay also because it is seen that this is also just a passing thought/emotion with less importance, except there is importance (lol), which just is accepted also. More "alertness"/"sharpness" and presence, except when there isn't, which is okay also.

No, no doubts at all ("strange," I didn't even notice this until you brought it up).

What is the most noticeable change?

For sure, the much more relaxed attitude towards life in general, "my own personality" (lol) or "way of being" of this character. Much more joy, without any reason, and much less worrying. Interestingly enough, it has also become much easier to speak my mind, to say no, as well as yes, which makes life, of course, much easier. It is more a surfing life's waves instead of fighting them and resisting them, more trust in the goodness of life.

What hasn't changed that you expected would change?

Still what is perceived as annoying noises—dog barking, children shouting, loud music (except my own, lol)—is arising and there is strong anger, with a felt painful body reaction. Still, no genius, and the girls are not waiting in line for me (just kidding). Oh! And no official notification that "I" am now an Officially Certified Enlightened Being, and that everybody, and life in general, would treat me with the respect due to that! (Not even animals seems to notice this—too bad!)

Of course, years back I had all kinds of fantasies about "waking up"/"enlightenment," or whatever we want to call it. I have come to learn that it hasn't anything to do with those fantasies at all. So, in a way, I could even say that "nothing has changed," while in another way "everything has changed." Strange, and, at the same time, not strange. I know that you understand. Oh, damn! I still have to pay taxes! So, this proves that I'm not enlightened yet—I need to work harder. LOL!

So, thank you, Ilona, you did a magnificent job! Or should I say, life, through the appearance of you, did a magnificent job? Hugging you right back, with a warm, thankful hug!

Ilona: I had tears of joy in my eyes reading this. What a journey! I'm truly delighted to hear the laughter! I am laughing with you!

Joyful, for no reason—that describes it, being, seeing, feeling love.

Thanks for the hug!

Much love.

Friederich:

I had tears of joy in my eyes reading this.

May I gently dry them? Thank *you*, Ilona. Yes, for sure it has been "quite a journey"! And then, has it really? LOL!

Ah, do you remember, Ilona, during our session on Skype, the situation with my dad? Well, I guess it was two or three days later, I actually called my dad and told him how much I loved him, and his reaction was very "touched," like, maybe surprised, or uncomfortable, and he said, "I love you too." It was very touching for me also, *very* important to have been able to let him know that (again), and I felt very joyful during and after that! So, I'm so thankful that that came up in our session, and that it opened up so beautifully!

I just thought that you may like to know that!

Ilona: That is wonderful! I'm very, very happy about this, heart opening.

Some time later, I asked Friederich how everything was going, and he told me that he had moved into a beautiful, nice and quiet place with the lovely sounds of birds chirping. Here is his response.

Dear Ilona,

Thank you for writing me, and, I'm doing wonderful! How did I get so wonderfully lucky?!

How it all looks for me now? The same, and not the same. A lot more appreciation and gratitude for whatever is, even the so-called bad stuff. I'm just no longer willing to separate life into good and bad. I have developed an appreciation for everything! And, of course, and as you well know, this is a lot of the time easier said than done. So what! I mean, it's in my awareness anyway, so why not appreciate it? Whatever bothers me may not go away (at least not always instantaneously—although in the end "This too will pass"). At least it's more enjoyable and, for whatever good it is, "it makes more sense to appreciate than to hate or plainly reject."

I keep reading, even the Law of Attraction stuff, and I've learned that while we consciously are only aware of fifteen bits of information per second, our unconsciousness is aware of fifteen million bits of information, so, in my "humility" (please don't laugh—LOL), I choose to acknowledge that maybe, just maybe (LOL), I don't have the full picture, and maybe, just maybe, there is something wiser and more intelligent and more all-knowing going on. I mean, it's really just a matter of "having it easier, being easier with myself, others, and life as such." One could even say that I have become wiser. Who would have thought that! Lol!

Definitely much more loving, humorous, and patient—except when not! Like this afternoon: I just burst out, "Shut up!" Did it hurt? Yes! Even my sincere apology was being rejected, but it definitely doesn't last for so long.

Curiously enough, having discovered my nonexistence hasn't made me less accountable or responsible. Quite the opposite! There is suddenly a power present that loves to be accountable and responsible. This is, at least for me, especially surprising, since when I first started getting interested in non-duality, I felt immediately powerless, and got to know quite a few "non-duality people" who were just plain mean, reckless, and heartless. The way I see it now, those people, like myself at that time, had a twisted mental concept.

Health is greatly improving, I'm even feeling quite confident that my health will be fully restored, in time. I have found a new passion for life which had been gone for several years (with occasional flickering ups, just to disappear again). With the passion having returned, there is also a broader interest in life—curiosity!

I'm still aware of a lot of anger, hatred, judgment, resentment, mistrust, and frustration somewhere deep down but, for whatever reason, it doesn't much bother me; it's like "No big deal!" I'm feeling rather confident that this too will pass!

A strange fear of beautiful women is also still present, but it's the same with the above-mentioned emotions—an attitude of "So be it," until it is.

Any advice for a reader? Not to buy this book! You, of course, know that I am just kidding. What comes to my mind is:

Dear Reader,

You can trust the loving guidance of Ilona. Everybody's experience is different, but this has been my experience. I was even so angry and full of hatred and frustration that I didn't want to live anymore. Ilona didn't talk me out of it, or invite me to change my beliefs about life, myself, or others. And, I may say that she is, in a truly lovely but firm way, relentless! She didn't give up on me, and believed in the truth (of no "me"). For this, I'm truly grateful!

How did I get so wonderfully lucky?

Ah, I'm now doing *ho'oponopono* and find it truly beneficial!

Love and peace!

And please, let me know if you see some other ways to support you and your possible readers!

Friederich

Marty

I'll let Marty introduce himself with this account he wrote, early in our correspondence, of how the seven steps (which I'll describe in the next chapter) worked for him and his wife.

My discovery of Liberation Unleashed (LU) came through a recommendation by a friend, during a telephone call. My friend hadn't yet been on the site for himself, but was told it was worth checking it out. Following that lead, I went onto the site and had a browse around. I was so impressed that I decided to buy the *Gateless Gatecrashers* book. I became engaged very quickly with the guiding encounters as they unfolded, becoming fascinated with how differently people responded to their tasks.

After reading quite a few accounts, I felt that I was beginning to get the hang of the process, and I began to look for my own responses before reading the responses the seekers gave. Over the days, I began to feel that I was beginning to get it. I was beginning to see for myself that there was no self, only a story, assumptions, and labeling. Often I would just stop whatever I was doing and just break out into a big smile. There was a growing sense of lightness and fun along with a keen engagement with the process of looking. It became the central feature of my life.

I remember sitting in a deck chair by the lakeside at Coniston, reading, looking, and responding. In one of the accounts, the seeker was nearly there, but was stuck on seeing there was no one in charge. He needed one last push. The push was something like, *Imagine that there* is *no one in charge, and live your day like that.*

That struck a chord with me, and as the day unfolded, it became clear to me that such indeed was the case. There is no one in charge. It all runs by itself.

Meanwhile, I had begun to share my impressions of the LU site, the *Gateless Gatecrashers* book, and the Direct Pointing process with my wife.

As Meg and I walked along the shore of Lake Coniston and up onto Torver Common, we talked about the LU site. Meg particularly wanted to explore the place of ethics and compassion in this Direct Pointing process.

Meg decided to get the book on her Kindle and read the accounts of the guided gate crashing. As she read, she began to take notes on what the guide had to say. In fact, she had only gone partway into the second account when she stopped reading.

In one of our discussions, usually sitting after breakfast, I had said that there was more work still to be done. Meg's response was to question that if things were unfolding after seeing no self, why did I feel there was work to be done? It was a question asked in all innocence, but it showed me that the Gate wasn't completely crashed. Something had snagged! Maybe the next step was to go on the LU site for help.

However, I had noted in the articles that Ilona had written a self-help guide: "Seven Steps to Liberation" [see the chapter "Seven Steps" later in this book]. I printed these off and suggested to Meg that we go through the steps together. I wanted to go through again, as I felt that something had snagged on the Gate. I wasn't there yet. I would be both a guide and a buddy on the mission to crash the Gate.

It so happened that we had a week free of grandparenting and other duties. We would do our intensive inquiry, taking as long as needed. We would give a day or more to each step, and proceed to the next step when we felt ready.

Each morning, after breakfast, we would read through Ilona's pointers and inquiry tasks, discuss and clarify them, and then set off on a long walk. We took the appropriate page with us, and often stopped to reread and further clarify.

These walks were largely silent, except for stopping to discuss a point or to share a new insight. At some point, later in the day, usually after the evening meal, we reviewed the current step and decided whether we were ready to move on or devote another day, maybe absorbing or looking some more. We both reported that our mental states felt similar to being on retreat—expansive and positive.

And now, our Direct Pointing session:

Marty: Hi, My name is Marty, and I came through the Gate a month ago using Ilona's seven-step guide. I waited a while to feel settled into this new way of being, and to be certain I wasn't kidding myself. I would like to know my next steps. Is there anyone I can correspond with?

With much gratitude for the Liberation Unleashed, wonderful work.

Ilona: Hi Marty. Thank you so much for your e-mail. It is great to hear that the seven steps were what got you to look. We usually ask a few questions and invite those that cross the Gate to join the LU community on Facebook for continuous support and friendship.

Marty: Hi Ilona, I was delighted to get a reply from you in person. I am so grateful for what you do. This is a fantastic, amazing, uncomplicated gift of freedom you have made possible. What you have made possible has been the biggest thing in my sixty-seven years on the planet. In my years of searching, I have been a Catholic cleric and a Buddhist cleric without finding what I was looking for. Until now. So, yes please to questions. I'd really like to help others. A friend of mine (who is in the Buddhist order I used to be in) is in a care home with multiple sclerosis, and asked me to help him crash the Gate. He is really impressed with LU, and is ready to go. However, he finds it very hard to type; he feels he can't go for it on the LU site. I started looking at the seven steps with him, but thought I'd better check in with you first.

PS: I had started an account of how the seven steps worked for me and my wife!

At this point, Marty sent me the account he'd written.

Ilona: Hi Marty, I'm delighted to hear that the seven steps were helpful for you and your wife. What a joy to share this journey with your loved one! Let's see if you are through with both legs. Here are the questions that we usually ask.

Please answer in full, when you're ready. Once you answer I will see if there are any sticky points. So take your time. As for your friend, you can guide him! There are also a few guides in LU that do that over Skype.

Sending love.

Marty: Hi Ilona, Thank you very much for getting back with the questions.

Yes, it was great to follow the seven steps with my wife—even when she sailed through while I snagged and got scared!

Thank you again so much for this gift.

1. Is there a separate entity "self," "me," "I" at all, anywhere, in any way, shape, or form? Was there ever?

No, nowhere. There is no self to be found in my experience, and I have looked and looked. I have looked. What I find is a big bundle of tendencies, thoughts, urges, all competing for attention. Yes, there is attention too, but that isn't an entity. There still arises a desire to control, to manage, but that's all it is, a desire—even an urgent desire at times. But that's all it is. There is no self, and what a relief! I am so happy to be rid of the burden created by that belief. No one to defend, even though the thought, the wish to defend, comes up. There is no one to promote and show off, even though the wish to be admired still shows up. There is no "I," even though I use the word all the time. I know that the "I" that I refer to is just the way we talk, because that's how language works. There is no self in anyone else either, and that's so fascinating. We are all big bundles of urges and tendencies, and anything can happen! It's so much more relaxed with my grandchildren, and kids I teach art to in school. No need to be so heavy about behavior, no one's setting out to do anything on purpose. It all just happens in the moment. A kid gets a bit excited, he or she needs reminding, but it just happens, and it's nobody's fault. No big deal.

There never was a self here in me or in anybody else. The creating of the self that we all have done is nobody's fault either. That's just what happens.

2. Explain in detail what the illusion of a separate self is, when it starts, and how it works from your own experience. Describe it fully as you see it now.

The illusion is an act of creating that we all do as we grow up in families, in school, in society. Maybe there is no other way for people to learn how to get what they want and to fit in with family and society at the same time. My grandchildren are home educated and are hardly ever sanctioned, but they still create a clamoring self in order to compete with siblings. So, I'm thinking that it's pretty much inevitable that children learn to do that. Especially when they start to say "I want…"

I can't remember early childhood, but I do remember having the desire to be accepted along with the desire to keep myself separate. I think maybe that's the dynamic that creates the sense of self.

Looking to my experience now, I can see how that desire to defend, to promote myself, to look out for my advantage is still there as a default bunch of impulses that pop up quick as a flash. Now, those impulses don't have anything to hang on to. I see them, and they just drift off. I certainly recognize that as a falling away of stuff of its own accord.

My wife tells me that I'm not reactive now. She doesn't have to worry about upsetting me. She can tell me challenging things in a straightforward way. That's my feeling too.

3. How does it feel to see this? What is the difference from before you started this dialogue? Please report from the past few days.

It feels so different and at the same time so ordinary and matter of fact. As it's been about five weeks since I saw there was no self, I've had time to absorb and to check out my experience. At first, I felt I couldn't really be sure. Had it really happened? Was I kidding myself? Were things any different at all? But then, things began to fall away. First of all, a heavy sense of guilt that had been dogging me for over twenty years just evaporated. That was the guilt about breaking up from my wife and kids and starting another relationship. I thought I was going to take that to my grave and now it's gone. The next thing I noticed was that a habit of mentally picking on my adopted daughter, for all sorts of things, just started to fall off. I just began to leave her be, she's just her own bundle of tendencies. No need to try to control any of that. Then my obsessive eBay habit of looking for windsurfing stuff began to fall off too. I would log on and look lots of times a day, every spare moment I had. And that just started falling off. What I have now is just more internal space, where I am happy with a strong sense of, *this is just right, here and now.*

I did spend quite a lot of energy looking at Buddhism again, and I wondered if my seeking compulsion was still there, and that I hadn't crashed the Gate after all. But that seems to have found its level now.

What I do find is that unpleasant feelings such as anger, anxiety, and fear are *so* much more visceral, so it's not like it's all happy-clappy. Nevertheless, there is a sense of deep peace and confidence that the way forward will just show itself.

4. What was the last bit that pushed you over? What made you look?

I had found the LU site through a friend, bought the book and raved about it to my wife. She began to read the book. I found your steps on the site, and we decided to have a go.

Following the seven steps with my wife was great fun…until step five. When it came to looking to find if there was a separate self, I began to become really frightened. Meanwhile, my wife (who is pragmatic, and had no expectations) just saw, with some tears, that there was no separate self. When I felt stuck and upset that evening, she remembered what you said about going back to expectations if you get stuck. So, I went back to look at my expectations and saw that I had big "Buddhist Insight" type expectations about the death of self. However, I still felt stuck in being too frightened to go on. I realized I needed just to be honest and honor the fear, bow to it, trust it, and just stay with the process. I still felt really disappointed. Next morning, I woke up with the simple certainty that the self is just a myth. No big feelings, just that simple truth. The self is a myth. It's just a story.

So, what pushed me over was seeing that I needed to honor my fear and acknowledge my unhelpful expectations. Then seeing just happened by itself, no effort, maybe when I was asleep!

5. Do you decide, intend, choose, control events in life? Do you make anything happen? Give examples from your experience.

This for me has been a biggie. The final place I found as the refuge for the belief in a self was in being the controller. The story I had been telling myself was that no matter how varied my life circumstances, I had been in control. In my many years as a class teacher, I had prided myself in having a lovely system of control. As a practicing Buddhist teacher for years, I had taught the central role of volition in creating karma: Do battle with the root poisons. Overcome the self. And so on and so on.

I see that the belief in a controller is such a big lie. There is no one in control. It's all an illusion. There are thoughts of wanting to control; there are really urgent, even painful feelings of wanting to control. There is even identification with the thought *I am in control*. But that's all there is. That's how nature works, how evolution works, how survival works. And it works for survival. But there is nobody doing that. It's all nature's programming doing its job really well.

Do I intend anything? No "me" needed to intend. Intending, organizing, knowing when a task is complete, when a need is met is all there in the program. Even my hens can do that when they lay their eggs.

All the things in my life, like getting to school on time, looking after the kids, all happen because the habits and tendencies are all there, making it all work smooth as clockwork.

Even in the higher order, events happen by themselves. Going on LU, reading the gatecrashing book, reflecting, looking for a self: these happen by themselves. Now that is an amazing miracle—new ideas, new contacts, LU guidance, all just happening, unfolding all by themselves. It's just a wave of energy and tendencies all bundling along.

What a relief! That burden is more and more being laid down. I don't have to worry about control, or make others feel they need to exercise control. It feels so much more like play.

6. *Anything to add?*

Ilona, I'm aware that all this might sound a bit euphoric, a bit too much like a big conversion high, but it's been five weeks now, and the falling off has been steady and incremental. In many ways, I feel that life is just the same as before. I often forget this central awareness of no self, being involved where I am and in what I am doing, in being anxious, fearful, excited about success, but the awareness seems to come back quite quickly, and the deep sense of peace with it. This is such an amazing gift. The greatest gift. Look, I've gone euphoric again!

That's it so far, Ilona. I just sat down and wrote this straight off without reflecting or correcting, in the belief it would more easily show any gaps or snags, or caught legs.

With much gratitude, Marty.

Ilona: Hi Marty, Thank you for the answers. They were delightful to read! I'm very happy for you and your wife—what a joyful turn of events. You have each other to share support on this journey—so beautiful. I can see from your answers that the Gate was crossed with both legs. Great! And of course it's just a beginning, a fresh start, there is much to explore. I'd love to invite you to Facebook groups. Could I post our conversation on my blog? It may be helpful for someone else. I can use your name or whatever name you prefer. Much love to you both. Huge smile.

Marty: Hi Ilona, I am thrilled to get the thumbs-up from you. I have been nervous, waiting to hear from you! I have tears in my eyes as I write. I cannot stress enough how grateful I am to you for this wonderful gift. Yes, very happy to have our conversation available under my name. Yes, I'd love to go on the site on that link and find my way around. I'd love to help others, and would like some help and training on that.

Much love and gratitude, Marty.

Ilona: You are most welcome! I love to hear that you are interested in sharing this gift with others. This is the biggest gift to me,
when you pass it on. It makes this work spread and frees people's
minds from confusion. What can be a bigger gift than freedom?

Much love to you and your wife.

I received the following from Marty after a little time had passed.

Since the Gate…

I crossed the Gate about six weeks ago now, and there have been a
few times when it crossed my mind, *Did it really happen?* Maybe I
made it up! Doubt about the crossing arose several times.

Perhaps the most frequent trigger has been, *So, I haven't changed that
much. I'm still having feelings I don't want, boredom, anxiety, irritation.*

The triggers have been linked to some unreal expectations I still
carry, lurking out of sight: expectations of becoming a much-
improved person. It's interesting to recollect that I needed to face
unrealistic expectations when I got stuck at the Gate (stage five of
the seven-step guide).

When doubt arose, a few things helped me: When I check, I am
sure, for certain, that there is no self. And that was what I set out to
discover. So, no doubt about the truth of that. So, the doubt has
been about the effects of crossing, rather than the "event" of crossing. However, when I look at what *has* changed, I am in no doubt
that the changes have been significant and not faked. For a start,
some of the changes were a surprise. Some very old feelings of guilt
have evaporated. I am much more patient with demanding little
grandchildren. Addiction to eBay searching has vanished. What's
more, these changes have been quite gradual, not driven by decision, so they are much more reliable. The change to how I see the
world around me has been *mega.* I have also benefited from reading
and reflecting on articles on LU. Particularly, the "After the Fall"
article by Scott Kiloby. But of most significance, I am in contact

with people who have crossed the Gate, and benefit hugely from chatting and checking things out. I am really transparent with these friends. I "tell on myself," as Scott would say. (I had the delight of guiding one of these friends, using the steps.) This kind of after-Gate support is so helpful.

So, the single piece of advice I would give is: make contact with other Gate crossers.

Six months later…

For some time after the Gate I felt the urge to review my relationship with Buddhism, and to reread some key texts. Was I a Buddhist after all? What I did find was that I recognized at once what those texts were saying when it came to recognizing no self. Only now, it seems so clear and simple, and without any need for further supporting beliefs or special practices. Now, it so happened that when I resigned some years ago from the Triratna Buddhist Order, I had kept my Buddhist name of *Adiccabandhu*. As a result of going through the Gate, I could see that I hadn't quite let go of my identity as a member of a Buddhist order, even though I had left the order some years ago. I returned to full use of my birth name, Marty.

These recent months since the Gate have seen a change in my relationships. It has become more and more clear to me that transforming relationship is what life is about!

During our long walks, Meg and I occasionally review how things have been for us since the Gate, and it has been great to do that. We are blessed with a harmonious relationship, and that seems to have become even more easy.

My relationship with my five grandchildren has continued to evolve more and more into a "going with the flow" style. What has surprised me is that I feel the occasional misunderstanding or disagreement with them very keenly. It really hits me in the gut. I guess the consequence is that I am far more careful when I feel reactive to some perceived slight!

My friendships have certainly been affected. Any friend who seems like he or she could be interested in liberation gets a copy of *Gateless Gatecrashers* and a print-off of Ilona's seven steps. So far, I have guided three of my friends. I am touched by the trust that these friends put in LU and in my guiding, and the result has been an even deeper friendship, with lovely communication between us. What greater gift can you give a friend? But the gift is also to myself. In guiding others, I revisit for myself the seven steps. And in so doing, come across a deeper and deeper realization of how things run.

Right now, my current realization is that all meaning is imagined. All my relationships, all my activities, are based on an imagined world, on my own worldview. My world is constantly built on interpretations of direct experience in the moment. And that is so amazing, what the mind can do. It can imagine anything!

So, the liberation process is still unfolding for me on a day-by-day basis. I know now that all I need do is just simply stay with my experience as it arises, with an increasingly easy acceptance of the imperfections that are bundling along as *me*. And, likewise, with an increasingly easy acceptance of the imperfections that are bundling along as friends, family, and people around me.

All the while, I have continued to read books about liberation and watch various online recordings. There is certainly a lot of awakening going on in the world right now. What I find is that none of the books or the online recordings match LU for clarity and directness.

While some liberated people describe their way to seeing with warmth, their accounts don't offer a bridge to cross. Others offer exercises that seem to have no effect.

It seems to me that LU goes straight to the core, without any grand claims or a need to stand on some holy ground to break through. You just get to see as clear as day that there is no self. No frills, plain and simple!

So, personally I would recommend anyone who seriously wants to be liberated to go for the direct LU approach.

Seven Steps

As more and more people came to me with an intention to look, I decided to put a basic map on my blog; I called it the "Start Here" page. I outlined the steps that I had noticed in the looking process. People followed them, and for some the steps were enough for them to *see*. If you are working with these steps, you can follow their order or not. The point is to verify what is true in experience—your experience. It is more important to describe what *you* see as true than to agree or disagree with what the steps suggest. If going through the steps is uncomfortable, you are doing them correctly. Intensity is part of this process.

These steps are guidelines only. The journey is taking you for a ride, and life is the best guide—all that is not in harmony will come up as tension. Your reactions to suggestions will show you the way forward and outline ideas that you are holding on to. Shoulds and should nots that come up will show blockages in the way. When stuck, always come back to expectations. They are distortions hiding and protecting beliefs. When the path is cleared and readiness is ripe, seeing happens.

You will need a pen and paper or whatever medium for recording that you prefer.

It's important to remember to look, to follow the pointers, to investigate, and to write down what you feel to be true.

Step One: Clearing the Path—Meeting the Fear

Here you are, ready to begin. Write this down:

There is no separate self at all in reality—no agent in charge, no manager, no watcher, no owner of life; all there is, is life flowing freely as one movement, one reality, one life, one nature, one intelligence, one god, one flow, whatever word resonates most. The separate self, or "I," is an illusion; there never was such an entity and never will be.

What happens when you allow this thought in? What comes up? Is there fear? Is there doubt? Resistance? Frustration? Something that wants to scream and make you turn away? Something that says this is not working? Or maybe there is feeling of wow, joy, or relief?

Watch, wait, notice, and write!

Notice all that is going on inside and just put it down in writing. Note what bodily sensations show up.

… … … …

Done? Okay. Bring it all closer.

If there is fear? Focus on the fear. Ask it to come closer.

Notice that it's a protection mechanism. The fear itself is like a door; it keeps you from looking behind the door. But it's just fear. On closer inspection, it is a certain sensation in the body. Look for it now. It's okay for it to be here; it is only a sensation, and it is doing its job of warning against danger. Something is there feeling the threat, and it is being protected. Just let fear be there. Honor it. Acknowledge its presence with respect and gratitude. Check to see where you feel it physically in the body. Notice the sensations.

Ask these questions and watch what comes up:

What is the fear itself?

What is it protecting?

What needs to be protected?

What is it that feels threatened?

Ask the fear (literally) to reveal why it's here. Ask it what it is trying to tell you; ask the fear to share its wisdom. What does it want to tell you?

If there is no self and never was, then there is nothing that needs to be protected.

Honor the feeling. Bow to it. Thank it for doing its job so perfectly. Notice that it is here to protect; it's a friend. Fear is really love in disguise. It is only showing you where to look. Fear points to the dark areas that need to be explored. Fear is not meant to be feared.

Now look behind the fear.

Is there anything behind it?

If so, what? And what is behind that?

What do you find?

If the mind gets blank, silently notice that the silence is not the absence of an answer, it *is* the answer. Let that sink in.

Done?

If you passed this stage and saw that there is nothing behind the fear, you are ready for the next step. If the fear is strong, if it feels like panic or terror, you may refer to the chapter "Fear Is a Sensation." It can help you to investigate fear more closely. You may also use the emotional freedom technique (EFT), which you can find online, to reduce the intensity to a more comfortable level.

Step Two: Strip Away All Expectations

Just write all your answers out and examine them. Your full honesty is key here—find all the expectations and write them down, then look for the hidden expectations. The chapter "Expectations Are Like Clouds That Cover the Sunshine" may be of use here.

What do you expect liberation is going to be like?

What do you want from it?

How do you imagine an awakened human behaves?

What will liberation feel like?

What do you expect to be different from now?

What will liberation give you, and what do you hope for?

What do you not want it to be like?

Once you write out all of your expectations, accept that they get in the way of seeing with fresh eyes, and leave them behind in order to take a fresh look. If you continue to cling to your expectations, go back and reread the chapter "Expectations Are Like Clouds That Cover the Sunshine," then look at what is behind the expectations. What is *there* that feels threatened?

No matter what you expect, the reality of the situation is not going to be exactly as you imagined. Any time you feel stuck, come back to your expectations. If you think that something should be happening, but it isn't, there is an expectation behind the thought. Expectations are not useful when looking; they are in the way.

Once your list of expectations is complete, examine it: which expectation will be hardest to let go of?

What is it that wants things to be different? Are these expectations yours? What is it that you are trying to hold on to?

What is, is simply here. Thinking makes this appear complex, when all is very simple.

Once you have dealt with fears and expectations, you can start exploring the next step.

Step Three: Get in Touch with the Real

Now it's time to get in touch with the real. By "real" I mean the direct, immediate experience that is happening versus the imagined.

By "real" I mean that which is actually here and does not disappear if you stop imagining and believing in it. It's right here, right now, and it's what *is*.

Try this exercise.

Try This for Yourself   Close your eyes.

Imagine that you are holding a spoon.

Imagine its form, size, weight, and temperature; feel the imaginary spoon as vividly as you possibly can for a few minutes.

Do this exercise before reading further.

… … … …

Open your eyes; is there a spoon here, in real life? Was there ever a spoon?

How did you see that there is no spoon?

What happened to the spoon?

Did it disappear or did it ever exist?

How about the sense perceptions you felt while imagining the spoon? Were they real? Were sensations happening?

Notice that there was no boom and no bright-light flashes in the eyes when you no longer imagined the imaginary spoon.

Look around the room and notice what is real. What is here now?

Can you see an absence of a spoon? Can you see "no-spoon" flying around? When you stop imagining a spoon, does something else replace it? A fork or something?

Here are another exercise.

Try This for Yourself Close your eyes and imagine you are in the kitchen. Just visualize and look around; notice where things are put. Notice the space, the feel of it.

See it in your mind's eye. This is an image: it can trigger feelings, contractions, expansions, thought stories and the feelings attached to them. Watch this triggering at play.

Open your eyes and see how an image can be created and explored in the mind. (This happens constantly. The mind is like a movie; scenes, scenarios, conversations, and memories are all playing out.)

Go to the kitchen and look at the same things that you saw in the image. How do imagining and experiencing the same things differ? Is the experience of the image of the kitchen and the experience of the actual kitchen the same?

What are the biggest differences?

Write down your observations.

Now for the fun part:

While standing in the kitchen, imagine a unicorn comes to visit. Say hello. Touch the horn, pat his back. Have a conversation with the unicorn about where he has been and how the kids are. Smile at this beautiful creature.

Then have a *look*. What happens to the unicorn when it's no longer imagined? Is there a "no-unicorn" here instead? Did the unicorn disappear?

Focus on the image of yourself, the separate, individual entity. Is it an image in the mind or something perceived via senses? Is there anything that may disappear?

When you have made the connection between what is imagined and what is not imagined but actually happening, explore each perceiving channel further. Can you see a self with eyes, hear it, touch it, smell and taste it? Can you find the self?

Is there an "I" or a "self" in touching, smelling, tasting, seeing, and hearing? Test it with each sense.

How and when is self experienced?

Is it constantly here or does it come and go?

Is there the sense of separateness right now, in this moment?

Is there a sense of oneness?

What is separate from what?

What do you find in experience right now?

What is limited, and by what?

What is here right now?

Look, not at an absence, but at what is actually here, happening right now.

Step Four: "I" Is a Thought—Thought Does Not Think

Contrary to what we have been fed since childhood, "I" is not a soul or a being; "I" is a thought. It is not a being, it is just a label. The word "being" should only be considered a verb, not a noun.

"I think, therefore I am." The simple meaning of this famous phrase, attributed to René Descartes, is that the simple act of someone wondering whether or not he or she exists is, in and of itself, proof that he or she does exist. At the very least, this phrase states that there is an "I" who does the thinking.

But let's not believe what somebody else says. Let's test it.

Close your eyes and find that which is always present.

A feeling of aliveness, an aware being-ness, an "I am."

Stay with the feeling.

Is it personal?

It feels personal because of all those years you thought you existed as a separate being.

In actuality, it is a sensation plus a labeling of the mind as "me."

Look at thoughts.

Where do they come from?

Can you control them?

What influences thoughts?

Do you know what your next thought is going to be?

Can you stop a thought in the middle?

Can you stop a thought from coming?

Can you think just happy, pleasant thoughts for half an hour?

Answer these questions for yourself, and notice the thinking process.

How do thoughts come?

In bundles, one after another, or one at a time?

Does one thought give birth to another?

Is the I-thought coming from a different place than all other thoughts?

Is "I" the thought or the thinker?

Notice that thoughts come and go by themselves. They are just thoughts and, like clouds in the sky, there is nothing that controls them; they roll one after another and there is no way to stop or get rid of them.

Look at the mind as a labeling machine. Experience happens, labeling follows. Noticing, observing, and witnessing happen, and labels pop up right after.

Write down what you notice about the thinking process. While writing, notice how a thought comes and the hand writes it down.

Is there a thinker?

Is there a reader?

To what do these thoughts rise?

Notice the body breathing.

Look. Is it breathing by itself or is there a breather?

The label says, "I breathe." Is there an "I" that does the breathing? How about when you sleep? Does breathing need a breather?

Examine simple and ordinary actions, like walking, eating, listening, and dancing. Every experience is followed by an "I did this" commentary. But look closer: Is there a walker, an eater, a dancer? If language says that there is a subject or object doing action, is that true in your direct experience?

Play with the labeling for a bit. Notice that "I" is a label, a word that precedes other words in the English language structure. Right now reading happens effortlessly, and if you just stop for a second, thoughts appear and start labeling. "I" is one of the thoughts.

Dig deeper:

Can a thought think?

Can a thought do anything?

So, if "I" is a thought and thought does not think, *where is the thinker?* Is there one? "I think, therefore I am," can now be broken down to:

"I" is a thought itself.

"I" does not think.

There is no "I."
Thinking happens.
By itself.

Step Five: There Is No Separate Self at All in Reality

Check it:

Is there a gap between the experienced and the experiencer? Is there an experiencer, a center to which life happens?

It's a good idea to get out into nature at this point in the process. Watch the sky, trees, animals, babies, and other people. See how everything moves and wiggles, including tree branches, grass, animals, birds, humans, thoughts, feelings, and sensations. Notice that the thoughts that arise are dependent upon what is being noticed, what is being experienced. See how attention moves freely, noticing whatever stands out the most. Life "lifeing" is one big orchestra of happening.

Watch life, aliveness, and how everything is flowing effortlessly. Expand your focus. Notice how everything simply *is*. Perceiving is happening. It's here, now, alive.

Notice how the word "seeing" can be called another word, such as "color." *Seeing color* is what we call "seeing."

There is no one behind the eyes, no watcher, no observer; there is only watching, only observing happening in the present moment. There is no agent that switches seeing on and off at will. The mind is doing its usual business of labeling experience, and it is doing so by itself, without effort.

When you look at what is looking, what is there?

Don't try to fit that which *is* into the frame of what you think you should be seeing. Don't make this about happy, relaxed feelings or a state of bliss. Notice what is actually happening. It may as well be frustration, tension, confusion, or seeking to realize something. Notice that, with closer inspection, it's a sensation that is being felt.

This is what is actually happening, including the story about the sensation.

The thing is, you are seeing this already. If there is doubt, notice that. Look right at it, see it for what it really is—another mechanism of protection. Just that. It is just a thought that arises and passes away. Keep looking at the obvious. Focus. Is there a focuser? Or is focusing happening?

You are seeing it already at this point; all that is needed to recognize this fully is noticing that it's already the case.

At this point there is nothing that you need or can do. Let it unfold. There is no agent that can let this unfold. See that there is no one who can do anything. No one to let this happen. No one to even surrender. It all just happens, with and without your consent. It's all happening already—noticing, recognizing, seeing. Trust that what is, *is*.

There are many traps here, and you may need to focus hard. Everything that is not direct looking is a distraction from looking. The mind may be creating all kinds of distractions, but just remember to hold focus.

At this point, if you need help, please visit the Gate Forum at http://www.liberationunleashed.com, where you can get help from our dedicated team, free of charge. Having somebody to talk about this is priceless.

At this point in the seven steps, you either see that you see it or you think that you don't see it.

The Bahiya Sutra (see http://awakeningtoreality.blogspot.sg/2008/01/ajahn-amaro-on-non-duality-and.html) puts it all so simply and clearly. Play with it. Spend time with it. See the world through this lens.

> *In the seen, there is only the seen,*
> *in the heard, there is only the heard,*
> *in the sensed, there is only the sensed,*
> *in the cognized, there is only the cognized.*
> *Thus you should see that*

indeed there is no thing here;
this, Bahiya, is how you should train yourself.
Since, Bahiya, there is for you
in the seen, only the seen,
in the heard, only the heard,
in the sensed, only the sensed,
in the cognized, only the cognized,
and you see that there is no thing here,
you will therefore see that
indeed there is no thing there.
As you see that there is no thing there,
you will see that
you are therefore located neither in the world of this,
nor in the world of that,
nor in any place
betwixt the two.
This alone is the end of suffering.

Step Six: How Does It Feel to Crash the Gateless Gate?

Has anything changed in normal everyday situations? Are there any changes in ordinary everyday activities? What hasn't changed at all?

Write it all down.

What is different now compared to before you started the investigation?

If you have passed through the Gateless Gate, it becomes obvious that there is no Gate. There is no "I" who needs to or can cross the Gate, and there never was. You may be glad to find that seeking has dropped away.

Answer this question: Is seeking still here?

If yes, what other expectations are there to let go of?

One thing is for sure, you are not going to hear angels singing, nor a sonic boom when you pass through the Gate. Doing so is just like seeing and recognizing that there is no imaginary spoon—there is a dropping of a belief. The shift can be very subtle, or it can come with intense bodily reactions and experiences; it does not matter how it is for others, how it happens for you is perfect for you in every way. Smooth or wild, it doesn't matter. What matters is that the assumption of a separate self drops away.

Step Seven: Falling

Right, step seven is when it gets interesting.

Since the core belief has been busted, a lot of lost beliefs will still be hanging around. Imagine a computer system: If you delete a program, there will still be files left behind that hinder the computer's performance, slowing it down. So what do you do? Defragment the system, tune it up, and clean up the files.

Knocking out the core belief is like a tsunami to the system. It leaves a lot of debris behind, a lot of corpses to take care of. What you want to do at this point is clarify, clarify, and clarify some more. Keep eyes open, let the beliefs surface. Keep looking. They will come up one by one ready to be examined and released. Don't fight them. Hold on to nothing. As soon as you start holding on to beliefs and ideas, you get stuck; you feel right about something and feel like you have an opinion. To unstick, just let it all fall off. That means question everything you are certain about.

I call this stage "falling" because all that is untrue falls away, and all that is true falls into place and starts making sense.

Some say it takes a few months to settle in, but everyone is different. So there is no way to know how long it will take for the system to reboot and rebalance. Faith in truth is your friend. Looking is the tool that has to be used over and over again. A burning desire to get the last bit of I Virus out of your system is another friend, as is a readiness to let go of everything that does not serve anymore. Doubt your precious beliefs and keep investigating. This is only a beginning, not an end. You have not crossed the Gate of happy ever after; no, the Gate is a tiny first step, a very important one, but not a final one by any means. Crossing the Gate is only a step over a line—an imagined one at that.

Look closely at the most precious beliefs that are close to the heart, in the no-touch zone. They are the ones that you really want to inspect up close. You will recognize them by feeling resistance. Follow resistance. It is here to let you know that another bit of the lie is sitting somewhere waiting to be noticed.

When the sticking point is removed, life becomes easier; there is a real sense of freedom, appreciation, effortlessness, trust, and awe. There is freedom in every situation. There is freedom to express without feelings of guilt, of fear, or of being wrong. "Freedom" does not mean you are free *from* a negative situation, but that you are free *within* the situation, free to experience fully whatever life brings. When you feel free, you no longer look at life through the lens of "me." Instead it's wide open, ready to be explored. Freedom may be an end to seeking, but not an end to exploring.

There are many traps, and one can get stuck in ideas and concepts.

Even the idea of no self can become another belief, a new identity. One can go to extremes and start building a new belief castle based on no self. To avoid this, keep looking, keep checking. What is here right now, right this moment? Where is this no self? Did it replace the self? Has Santa been replaced by "no-Santa"?

As soon as you are convinced of something labeled "truth" and convinced of how things are, you are stuck in concepts. As soon as there is knowledge, there is believing in stories. Knowing and knowledge are not the same. After realization happens, there is a lot of unknowing that follows. There's a falling away of the old, while the new is falling into place; then the new falls off as well.

There is no end to falling. In the beginning it can be intense. It all depends on how easy it is for you to let go of holding on. There is no one to hold on, but grasping still happens. Falling continues, there is no landing place, no solid ground to hit. Eventually it smooths out and one relaxes into it and learns to fly.

So What?

Nothing changed, but everything looks different. If this make sense, then the Gateless Gate was crashed, the illusion of separate self is seen through. The nonexistent line is crossed and there is no way back.

The End of the Search, but Not the End of Our Exploring

Crashing the Gate may be the end of seeking, but it is not the end of exploration. Seeking may not stop immediately; it may still have momentum. The recognition of no self is just the beginning of seeing life and "your self" in a new light. It takes time to clean up all the mess, to settle in and adjust. The journey continues, the story carries on, but thoughts have been seen to be thoughts. The story is no longer solid, true, or real.

"So what?" you might ask. You may still feel like a separate being, but now you have the ultimate tool: looking! So keep on looking. Keep noticing, keep asking questions. Keep finding silence, being, and presence, and rest in them. All you need is already here. Trust that life is unfolding by itself and that there is no other way than this.

You will know when deconstruction is over. Until then there is work to do. By "work," I mean two things:

Question what you know is true.

Rest in being.

Some Things Change Quickly, Others May Take Longer

There is so much to explore, and life will bring all that wants to be seen into the present moment. So whatever shows up is here to be looked at. Say yes to it all. See everything as an opportunity to deepen. Question everything, and little by little you will notice changes in everyday life: less judgment, more openness; less thinking, more appreciation; less story, more being; less structure, more flow. You will notice that some habitual thoughts no longer arise. The story changes in a way that allows more space for simply being.

There might still be expectations, confusion, and doubt. That's normal at this stage. You may be wobbling between "I get it" and "I don't get it." You may be thinking that this is not enough, that some experiences need to happen, that you should be happy and blissful all the time.

When these thoughts arise, bring the focus to what is here now. There is no other time or space. Just this. And look again: what is here that wants this to be different, and what feelings are here about that? Come back to stillness.

The search may be over, but the journey continues. This is an opening, an invitation to look deeper, to free the mind from conditioned patterns, to become aware of habitual thinking, to unhypnotize yourself from the dream of separation. This is where you start living authentically, spontaneously, and are okay with all that comes. This is where you rediscover the beauty of being.

Don't Hold On to Anything

My only advice at this stage is to hold on to nothing. Don't hold on to anything.

When beliefs start falling, when certainty is no longer there, it may be scary and painful, but all of this is part of the cleaning-up process. Bring attention to the here and now, notice what is happening, rest in being, and, at the same time, question all beliefs—one by one.

You may look into time, world, body, emptiness, awareness, space, impermanence...the list continues, and wonder what these things are. There are many great teachers who offer different ways to explore. I would like to mention Adyashanti, Greg Goode, Rupert Spira, Byron Katie, and Alan Watts.

I highly recommend connecting with others who have crossed the Gate, in person or online. Sharing your experiences and getting support when needed is priceless. You will always be welcomed by the Liberation Unleashed community, where you will find people to talk to. Trying to explain looking to a friend or family member may be met with rolling eyes and resistance, so being able to connect with people who understand can be very helpful. If you feel lost, don't worry—it too shall pass.

Here and now, all is always as it should be. How to know that? It's already here. Isn't that wonderful?

You may now find that feelings are much more intense, unfiltered, and raw, or that emotions come up and pass quickly. You are free to feel, to experience, and to enjoy the intensity. It's juicy and makes you feel alive. The gift of freedom is being able to feel free to live life in its fullness, which includes all.

Pass the Message On

When I saw through the illusion, I went on Google and searched for quotes about enlightenment. It was remarkable that I could finally understand what they meant. The words of the sages and the Buddha finally made perfect sense. I came across these words attributed to Gantama Buddha:

> Not one or two, Subhuti, not one or two, but all beings, men, women, animals, birds, trees, rocks. All the beings in the world. One should create such a determination that I will lead all of them into nirvana.

The quote spoke to me. I felt that I had to ring the wake-up call. I knew that waking up and waking the rest, or at least as many as I could, was what I was here to do. I had finally found a way to help, and I had to share it with all. The fire in me would not let me rest until my call was heard. I kept ringing the bells, singing my song, writing the *Marked, Eternal* blog, talking to people on Facebook groups, making waves, getting banned from groups, joining others, and creating others. In the beginning, the rebellious spirit took over, and all I could think of was how to make more people see the simple and obvious: there is no separation from life itself.

I met Elena in one of the groups, and we became best friends. A few months later, Liberation Unleashed was born, and more and more people started to join, having a look and seeing for themselves. It was exhilarating.

I had hundreds of dialogues on forums and through e-mail. Some days it took me a couple of hours to answer all of the queries. Slowly, the community emerged, and those who *saw* started to guide those who came to see. The message was heard and was passed on in all different ways. I have met many amazing people who inspired each other to carry on, who make *guiding* available for everyone. The movement took over and has been growing ever since.

I'm very grateful to all the people at Liberation Unleashed who dedicate their time to guide. It's a most beautiful gift that one can give, the gift of freedom. And I sincerely hope that one day, understanding separateness as a mind-created illusion will be a common-sense thing, and that we can all live in harmony and respect each other. It is my wish that acting out of love will replace self-centered egoic behavior, and that humans will come back to their natural-ness, in which peace is the norm and not some threat or unachievable goal. It seems there is a long way to go, but who knows what is coming.

If you find that realizing there is no separateness has had an impact on your life, then pass the message on and be a part of the ripple. Help your seeker friends find the way through the Gateless Gate. The more people who see this, the merrier. We are all in this together. What good is freedom if people next to us are suffering, right? This is no longer something for only the chosen ones; it is available for anyone who dares to look.

Thank you for taking this journey with me. I would like to hear from you about your journey and whether or not this book was helpful. If you feel a little stuck, please come to the forum at http://www.liberationunleashed.com, where someone will be able to help you.

I'll leave you here, as I have talked enough. Be well, and enjoy the ride as it takes you deeper into wherever it takes you.

Love,
Ilona

A Note of Gratitude

Thank *you* for taking this journey.

I would also like to use this opportunity to thank all the people who shared their process with readers. Thank you Nona, Sacha, Lakshmi, Shanti, Rowland, Friederich, and Marty.

A warm thank you to my husband, Narimantas, for keeping me grounded and giving me space to do this work. Thank you for all of the twenty years we have shared together, for your love, and for your support.

A huge thank you to Catherine Noyce and her husband, Julian, for making this book possible, and for taking care of many details that made this book what it is.

I have so much appreciation and so few words to express it. I bow in honor to all who inspired me, who pushed me to look further, who made me question what I thought was truth, and who opened my eyes and heart. The list is huge! I am forever grateful to Elena Nezhinsky, my best friend and inspiration; Pamela Wilson, for demonstrating how to gently untangle the knots; whomever wrote the Jed McKenna books, for cracking the foundation of the castle of lies and pushing me to deconstruct it brick by brick; and Ciaran Healy, for finishing the job with a single pointer. My deep gratitude to Julie Rumbarger, for helping me to join the pieces of this text into a whole, for fixing my broken English, and for being a beautiful friend.

I want to thank all the people who joined this movement and are helping one another, spreading the word, and guiding selflessly over the Internet and in person. Thanks to all the administrators who look after the LU forum and its groups.

The silent revolution has already begun. Thank you for taking part.

Afterword
by Elena Nezhinsky

I met Ilona in October 2010, online in one of the spiritual groups. A year later, Liberation Unleashed was born. It is fascinating how, when something new is about to come into existence, life always provides a vehicle for it. In this case, it was our meeting. We felt a genuine interest and respect for each other and, most of all, had a mutual wish to help people to end their suffering. We were adding to each other's strengths, fitting tightly for the one goal we had: to translate our own experience of awakening for others. We were looking for ways to make the process of guided inner inquiry as efficient as possible, and a process that could resonate with people of all ages and all varieties of life lived.

If I used an image to describe the creation of Liberation Unleashed and the first year of our work, it would be of fire. That fire was inside us; we were burning with a deep desire to help others to see—to see the truth of no separation. Ilona and I spent many nights talking to each other online because we simply couldn't fall asleep. The excitement of the work was too great for us to slumber. With each person we had the honor to work with, we often felt an outpouring of love and joy that lingered for many days after the inquiry was complete. We felt the possibilities of this work and its benefit to people, and we were riding a huge wave of expansion.

There were others there who supported the movement, and noticing the community growing around the world was overwhelming. I often had tears in my eyes thinking about what was really happening, thinking about all the people working with others self-lessly day and night, fitting this work in between family and day jobs.

The collaboration of Ilona and me in the beginning, and then others joining soon thereafter, made this method of looking into reality very efficient for the right type of seeker. This method is not something that either of us developed, nor is it anything new. Looking directly at reality and questioning one's beliefs about it is embedded in many spiritual and religious paths. It is often hidden behind years of preliminary work, the work that strengthens the character first before destroying it—that is, the illusion of it. It happened that this work, which we later called Direct Pointing, was in great need at the time, and still is. It just so happened that some of us were there, and the right match, to bring it forth for people who were asking for help to end their spiritual seeking.

People seeking on a spiritual path are the same, regardless of whether they live in Europe, the Middle East, Australia, Latin America, the United States, or Russia. Regardless of our nationality, education, profession, religion, or spiritual background, at some point we might become exhausted by the seeking, by the wish to constantly improve what we perceive to be ourselves and our lives. We start to doubt our tradition, path, or technique. We see that the more we seek, the more seeking ground is in front of us. We feel burnt-out on the path and start looking for a way out. Awakening is not a qualitative process, it is a quantum leap; it is a dying of the old ways of seeing; it is an opening of new perception. If one is ready to release old, habitual ways of looking at life, one is ready to make a leap. In Liberation Unleashed, we found where one should look and how one should look to release old ideas, so the leap would be possible. In this book, Ilona structured this method of inquiry with clear steps and instructions so that anyone, even those who don't have a guide or prefer to look alone, can start the work. Her work in this book is brilliant, and each step she presents has been tested by hundreds of people in one-on-one work by Liberation Unleashed guides.

Today Liberation Unleashed is an amazing community of volunteers around the world. They do their work online, in live meetings, and via Skype and telephone. What we all have in common is the same spark, a burning desire, to help anyone who is looking to see the selfless nature of being. Everything that works—what we have found, developed, and tested—is available in several books we published and at our forum, website, and blogs. All of the material we publish on the Internet is in the public domain. Please use it for your own benefit, to see the truth, and for the benefit of others. We are ever growing, and if you feel the desire to help in any way, be that guiding others or applying other skills in our community, we welcome you!

Please take each step very seriously. And may you be successful in this undertaking!

—Elena Nezhinsky

Ilona Ciunaite was born in Lithuania. Always interested in the mind and how it works, she has a degree in psychology and a mind-set to focus on freedom for herself and those who find her. Ciunaite lives in England with her husband Narimantas, a tattoo artist from whom she learned the art of tattooing. Together they run a custom tattoo studio in West Sussex (http://www.mantas-tattoo.com).

Ciunaite's search for truth started in 2002, when for the first time she "experienced silence of the thinking mind, a sweet sense of being, contentment, peace," and "feeling at home." In 2010, she discovered Jed McKenna's books, which were a shock to her belief system and catapulted her "out of hypnosis" and toward the realization that all she believed was not truth. It wasn't until the initial deconstruction was done, after months of painful self-inquiry, that Ciunaite felt at peace: there was an emptiness, a not knowing, a not believing anything about anything. Then the last step was taken and the separate self was seen to be an illusion. She started writing a blog, *Marked, Eternal*, where she shared thoughts about this new-found freedom and invited readers to look for themselves in their own experience. Later, Ciunaite and her friend Elena Nezhinsky helped develop a process called Direct Pointing, which consists of a dialogue between a guide and a seeker. In September 2011, the Liberation Unleashed website and forum was launched. Together Ciunaite and Nezhinsky published a book, *Gateless Gatecrashers*, that consists of conversations leading to self-realization, and which can be downloaded for free from the Liberation Unleashed website.

Liberation Unleashed is a global movement of people helping others to see through the illusion of self. Ciunaite has had hundreds of conversations with people from all around the globe. Her main focus and work is helping people end their seeking by inviting them to question their fundamental assumptions and look at their own experience. She does not give answers, only questions. In this way a seeker may see what is going on for themselves and free their minds from conditioned patterns to explore whatever comes next. Ciunaite holds live meetings and group sessions in the UK. All of her work can be found on her blog *Marked, Eternal* at http://markedeternal.blogspot .com and on The Gate forum at http://liberationunleashed.com.

MORE BOOKS from NON-DUALITY PRESS

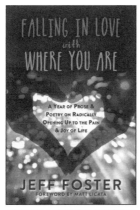

ISBN: 978-1908664396 | US $16.95

ISBN: 978-1908664242 | US $14.95

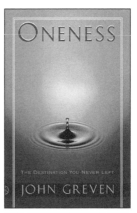

ISBN: 978-1908664297 | US $13.95

ISBN: 978-0955176203 | US $12.95

NON-DUALITY PRESS
An Imprint of New Harbinger Publications
www.newharbinger.com